T0215202

Lecture Notes in Computer Science

Lecture Notes in Artificial Intelligence   14317

Founding Editor

Jörg Siekmann

Series Editors

Randy Goebel, *University of Alberta, Edmonton, Canada*
Wolfgang Wahlster, *DFKI, Berlin, Germany*
Zhi-Hua Zhou, *Nanjing University, Nanjing, China*

The series Lecture Notes in Artificial Intelligence (LNAI) was established in 1988 as a topical subseries of LNCS devoted to artificial intelligence.

The series publishes state-of-the-art research results at a high level. As with the LNCS mother series, the mission of the series is to serve the international R & D community by providing an invaluable service, mainly focused on the publication of conference and workshop proceedings and postproceedings.

Shiqing Wu · Wenli Yang ·
Muhammad Bilal Amin · Byeong-Ho Kang ·
Guandong Xu

Editors

Knowledge Management and Acquisition for Intelligent Systems

19th Principle and Practice of Data and
Knowledge Acquisition Workshop, PKAW 2023
Jakarta, Indonesia, November 15–16, 2023
Proceedings

 Springer

Editors
Shiqing Wu (iD)
University of Technology Sydney
Sydney, NSW, Australia

Wenli Yang (iD)
University of Tasmania
Hobart, TAS, Australia

Muhammad Bilal Amin (iD)
University of Tasmania
Hobart, TAS, Australia

Byeong-Ho Kang (iD)
University of Tasmania
Hobart, TAS, Australia

Guandong Xu (iD)
University of Technology Sydney
Sydney, NSW, Australia

ISSN 0302-9743   ISSN 1611-3349 (electronic)
Lecture Notes in Artificial Intelligence
ISBN 978-981-99-7854-0   ISBN 978-981-99-7855-7 (eBook)
https://doi.org/10.1007/978-981-99-7855-7

LNCS Sublibrary: SL7 – Artificial Intelligence

This Springer imprint is published by the registered company Springer Nature Singapore Pte Ltd.
The registered company address is: 152 Beach Road, #21-01/04 Gateway East, Singapore 189721, Singapore

Paper in this product is recyclable.

Preface

This volume contains the papers presented at the Principle and Practice of Data and Knowledge Acquisition Workshop 2023 (PKAW 2023), held in conjunction with the 20th Pacific Rim International Conference on Artificial Intelligence (PRICAI 2023), from November 15–16, 2023, in Jakarta, Indonesia.

For the last two decades, PKAW has been a platform for researchers to share their ideas and engage in in-depth discussions about their work related to knowledge acquisition, which is a core area within the field of Artificial Intelligence (AI). The scope of PKAW is not limited to traditional knowledge acquisition approaches such as human (expert)-centric ones, but also covers diverse areas closely related to knowledge acquisition such as knowledge engineering, knowledge management, machine learning, data mining, etc. Over the past years, PKAW has covered a diverse range of topics that align with the advancements in AI research.

In recent years, AI has been unprecedentedly in the spotlight owing to its remarkable success in several industries, and presently, research on AI is entering an important stage in terms of how it will contribute to the forthcoming AI society. Among the numerous AI-related workshops conducted worldwide, PKAW primarily focuses on the multidisciplinary approach of human-driven and data-driven knowledge acquisition, which is the key concept that has remained unchanged since the workshop was first established. The recent approaches of AI, such as large language models, have demonstrated their superiority in many real-world applications. Nevertheless, training effective AI methods usually requires a massive volume of data. Even in the ongoing era of "big data," quite a few cases of data analysis come across scarcity of data because of the cost, privacy issues, and the sporadic nature of its occurrence. We believe that human-driven approaches, such as modeling the implicit knowledge of human experts, might be effective in such cases. Thus, a multidisciplinary approach is a much-needed breakthrough for the efficient integration of AI-based advanced research for the upcoming AI society. This is the direction that PKAW takes.

This year, we received 28 submissions and finally accepted 9 regular papers and 2 short papers. All papers were single-blind peer-reviewed by three independent reviewers. These papers demonstrate advanced research on machine learning, natural language processing, and intelligent systems.

These successes would not have been attained without the support of the people involved in this workshop. The workshop co-chairs would like to thank all the people who supported PKAW 2023, including the PKAW Program Committee members and sub-reviewers who contributed their precious time to review the submitted papers, and the PRICAI Organizing Committee, who appropriately dealt with our requests and all of the administrative and local matters. We thank Springer for publishing the proceedings in the Lecture Notes in Artificial Intelligence (LNAI) series. Further, we would like to extend a special thanks to all the authors who submitted their papers, presenters, and attendees.

November 2023

Shiqing Wu
Wenli Yang
Muhammad Bilal Amin
Byeong-Ho Kang
Guandong Xu

Organization

Workshop Chairs

Shiqing Wu   University of Technology Sydney, Australia
Wenli Yang   University of Tasmania, Australia
Muhammad Bilal Amin   University of Tasmania, Australia

Program Chairs

Byeong-Ho Kang   University of Tasmania, Australia
Guandong Xu   University of Technology Sydney, Australia

Publicity Chair

Yan Kong   Nanjing University of Information Science and Technology, China

Webmaster and Workshop Coordinators

Hai Huang   University of Tasmania, Australia
Yuhui Jin   University of Tasmania, Australia

Honorary Chairs

Paul Compton   University of New South Wales, Australia
Hiroshi Motoda   Osaka University, Japan

Advisory Committee

Quan Bai   University of Tasmania, Australia
Qing Liu   Data61, CSIRO, Australia

Maria R. Lee   Shih Chien University, Taiwan
Kenichi Yoshida   University of Tsukuba, Japan
Deborah Richards   Macquarie University, Australia

Program Committee

Xiongcai Cai   University of New South Wales, Australia
Wen Gu   Japan Advanced Institute of Science and
                                Technology, Japan
Huan Huo   University of Technology Sydney, Australia
Jianhua Jiang   Jilin University of Finance and Economics, China
Toshihiro Kamishima   National Institute of Advanced Industrial Science
                                and Technology, Japan
Matthew Kuo   Auckland University of Technology, New Zealand
Weihua Li   Auckland University of Technology, New Zealand
Lei Niu   Central China Normal University, China
Kouzou Ohara   Aoyama Gakuin University, Japan
Tomonobu Ozaki   Nihon University, Japan
Fenghui Ren   University of Wollongong, Australia
Kaize Shi   University of Technology Sydney, Australia
Shuxiang Xu   University of Tasmania, Australia
Takahira Yamaguchi   Keio University, Japan
Yi Yang   Hefei University of Technology, China
Dayong Ye   University of Wollongong, Australia
Tetsuya Yoshida   Nara Women's University, Japan
Zi-Ke Zhang   Zhejiang University, China

Additional Reviewers

Jiaqi Deng
Yuxuan Hu
Renjie Li
Xiang Li
Dingbang Liu
Haotian Liu
Shouxing Ma
Yikun Yang
Naimeng Yao

Contents

Predicting Peak Demand Days for Asthma-Related Emergency Hospitalisations: A Machine Learning Approach

Rashi Bhalla[1]([✉]), Farhaan Mirza[1], M. Asif Naeem[2], and Amy Hai Yan Chan[3]

[1] Auckland University of Technology, Auckland, New Zealand
rashibhalla25@gmail.com
[2] National University of Computer & Emerging Sciences, Karachi, Pakistan
[3] University of Auckland, Auckland, New Zealand

Abstract. Predictive analytics in the realm of health has taken on a critical role in disease prevention, particularly concerning prevalent ailments in society. The World Health Organization reports that asthma affected approximately 262 million individuals in 2019, resulting in 455,000 deaths. Each year, asthma-related concerns account for over one million visits to emergency departments, as highlighted by the American College of Asthma, Allergy & Immunology. For developing the model, we are using a configurable algorithm called Predicting Peak Demand (PPD) to anticipate days with elevated asthma-related Emergency Department (ED) visits and hospitalisations in Auckland, New Zealand. By leveraging diverse data sources, the model acts as a valuable planning tool for public health providers, particularly during periods of heightened demand, such as instances of overcrowding witnessed during cold weather or disease outbreaks like COVID-19. The PPD algorithm employed in this model effectively forecasts asthma-related hospitalisations. Meteorological factors, air quality data, and Google trends constitute the sources utilised in building the model. Comparative analysis was conducted using various machine learning algorithms, including ensemble modelling, with a dataset spanning 1,097 continuous days. Techniques like SMOTE and Random Over-Sampling were implemented to address class imbalance to generate synthetic data for the minority class. Experimental evaluation reveals that this model achieves an accuracy of approximately 91.00% in predicting peak demand days for asthma-related hospitalisations. The utilisation of this diverse data-driven model for predicting adverse events like asthma-related overcrowding at a population level can lead to timely interventions, mitigating the socio-economic impact of asthma.

Keywords: Asthma · Big Data · Classification · Data analysis · Emergency department · Heterogeneous data sources · Predictive modelling · Population health management

© The Author(s), under exclusive license to Springer Nature Singapore Pte Ltd. 2023
S. Wu et al. (Eds.): PKAW 2023, LNAI 14317, pp. 1–14, 2023.
https://doi.org/10.1007/978-981-99-7855-7_1

1   Introduction

Health is becoming a crucial issue in predictive analytics and focuses on the prevention of diseases that are commonly prevalent in society. Health forecasting, which includes risk prediction modelling, is a data-rich field that serves as a valuable tool for predicting health events or situations and forewarning future events. It has been commonly used for decision-making, particularly for Emergency Department (ED) visits, daily hospital attendances and admissions [12].

Asthma is one of the most prevalent and costly chronic conditions globally [4]. It accounts for more than 400,000 hospitalisations annually in the U.S., and these inpatient stays often come with physical and mental side effects [3]. New Zealand (NZ) is one of the countries with the highest prevalence and mortality rate due to asthma. Respiratory disease is NZ's third most common cause of death. Organisation for Economic Co-operation and Development (OECD) statistics indicate NZ has one of the highest hospital admission rates for asthma among OECD countries.

The prediction model for asthma can be broadly divided into two types; individual-level model and population-level model. The former type of model makes predictions for specific individuals, while the latter targets a sample of the population or community as a whole. There are several factors that trigger and exacerbate asthma, namely weather conditions, environmental factors etc. Generating a model leveraging diverse data sources to predict asthma-related ED visits and admissions at a population level would provide timely and targeted influences to minimise the socio-economic impact of asthma. Our research aims to exploit the distributed data sources to study the relationship between heterogeneous parameters and asthma-related hospitalisations, thereby using them for building up a prediction model by following the procedures outlined in the Predicting Peak Demand (PPD) algorithm. The diverse data sources examined in this study include meteorological parameters, air quality parameters, and search trends. Factors under each category are analysed for their relationship with asthma-related visits and admissions. The major contributions made in this research are summarised as follows:

- This study represents a preliminary step in the pursuit of forecasting population health trends related to asthma exacerbations in New Zealand.
- To enhance the prediction of asthma-related visits and admissions, novel parameters like black carbon and ultraviolet index were incorporated into the data sources, allowing an analysis of their impact on asthma-related healthcare utilisation.
- Data analysis was conducted to understand the correlation context between asthma episodes and environmental factors.
- The study employed a combination of deep neural networks and classical machine learning techniques to achieve its objectives.
- It demonstrates the applicability of utilising social media data in the development of health forecasting models.

– Furthermore, a lagged effect analysis was applied to investigate the delayed impact of parameters on asthma conditions, providing further insights into the forecasting model.

2   Related Work

A plethora of work has been undertaken for exploring and analysing the correlation of varying factors with asthma-related ED visits and hospitalisations [1,5,8]. Most of these studies focus on individual-based (personalised) models for asthma. A Poisson regression analysis has been applied in [2] to interpret the associations between paediatrics asthma-related ED visits and environmental factors in Washington, DC. These factors included daily temperature, mould count, diverse ranges of pollen, ozone, and air pollution measured in terms of $PM_{2.5}$. Further, it explored the patterns of asthma-related ED visits depending on socio-economic status and age groups. Moreover, the lagged effect was also examined for up to 4 days. The authors in [6] analysed the association between different air pollutants and ED visits for asthma in Indianapolis. This work also highlighted the comparative analysis among different seasons and age groups. The age group chosen for this study was greater than or equal to 5 years. This work also utilised Poisson regression in a time series framework to learn the correlation. The parameters identified as risk factors in this study were SO_2, Ozone, $PM_{2.5}$, temperature, humidity, and barometric pressure. The authors identified an association of risk factors with asthma for a lag of up to 3 days. These two studies focused on analysing the effects of various factors on asthma-related ED visits.

Not much work has been accomplished centring population-based prediction models for asthma. The authors in [11] have introduced a novel method in this direction that utilises multiple data sources for predicting asthma-related ED visits for specific areas in the United States in near real-time. The data sources used in this study were Twitter data, Google search interest, and environmental sensor data. The sensor data included data about the air quality parameter involving six types of pollutants. The work undertaken in this paper demonstrated the application of heterogeneous data mining for health surveillance. Authors have used Decision Trees, Naïve Bayes, SVM, and ANN as the classification method to produce the prediction model and compare their accuracy. The main limitation of this work was the short time frame of the study, consisting of only 74 days which lacked to examine the effects of seasonal variations. Secondly, this work missed the concept of analysing the lagged effect that may exist between changes in the Air Quality Index (AQI) and the number of asthma-related emergency visits.

Another state-of-the-art approach [9] focused on various weather and pollutant data in Dallas County of Texas to develop a forecasting tool for respiratory diseases, including Chronic Obstructive Pulmonary Disease (COPD), asthma, and other respiratory conditions. The study period in this work was 3 years, from 01/01/2011 to 31/12/2013, which included eight parameters covering weather and pollutant measurements. This study highlighted the usage of

Table 1. Existing similar work.

Year	Author	Location of study	Disease	Time Per.	Acc (%)
2015	S. Ram et al. [11]	Dallas, USA	Asthma	74 days	70
2018	K. L. Khatri et al. [9]	Dallas County, USA	All resp. dis	3 years	81

ANN classifiers and demonstrated good accuracy could be achieved using these measurements as the input variables. More insight provided details about the lagged effect of predictors on asthma-related visits and admissions. However, the study was confined to a limited number of predictors. The authors mentioned the capability of ANN to achieve correct prediction, even after learning from data with noise, and thus they didn't use any data cleaning technique.

However, the focus of this study lies in the development of population-based forecasting models specifically for asthma. Table 1 provides a summary of closely linked existing work.

3   Methodology

Developing a predictive model consists of several stages, starting from acquiring data from diverse sources to evaluating the final model. The diverse data sources examined in this study include *meteorological parameters, air quality parameters, and search trends*. Factors under each category are analysed for their relationship with asthma-related visits and admissions. Finally, a refined list of predictors is utilised to create a prediction model. Furthermore, a relative analysis has been generated comparing the performance of prediction models developed, using different machine learning techniques, *ANN, RF, SVM, XGB, and Ensemble Classifier*. Work has also been conducted for oversampling techniques like *SMOTE* [7] and *random over-sampling* [10], aspiring to procure a balanced classification problem. *Below is the list of all the stages:*

1. Data Collection
2. Data Preparation
3. Data Analysis and Feature Selection
4. Prediction Model

The diagrammatic presentation of all the stages has been presented in Fig. 1, and the detailed description of each stage has been covered below.

3.1   Data Collection from Diverse Sources

The first step towards prediction modelling commences with collecting raw data. In this case, apart from asthma-related hospitalisations, the model involves data from distinct sources, air quality parameters, meteorological factors, and Google Trends. The collected data were preprocessed, prepared, and refined. Finally, it was used for predictive modelling for asthma.

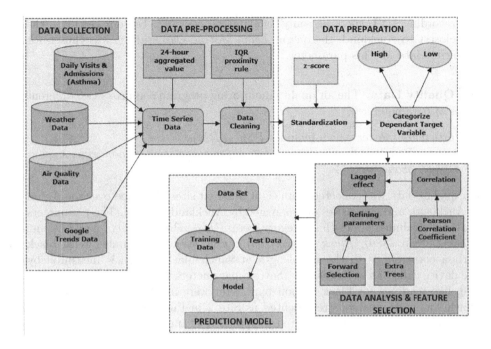

Fig. 1. Processing heterogeneous data sources for generating the forecasting tool.

Hospital Data. De-identified data for asthma-related admissions and ED visits were collected from Auckland Hospital, Auckland District Health Board (ADHB), which is now known as Te Toka Tumai under the new health entity Te Whatu Ora. Ethics approval for this study was obtained from *Auckland Health Research Ethics Committee*, AH22149, with an expiry date of 11/05/2024. The data for asthma was based on the International Classification of Disease Tenth edition -Australian Modification [ICD10-AM] codes *J45.2x to J45.90x, R05, R06.00-R06.2*. These classifications are used in the literature to identify asthma-related presentations to the hospital. This data accounts for daily counts of ED visits and admissions related to asthma for three years, starting from 1st Jan 2018 to 1st Jan 2021, forming a continuous data of 1097 days.

Meteorological Data. The data for the meteorological factors were collected from the National Institute of Water and Atmospheric Research, commonly known as NIWA. The list of parameters that were inspected for this study was: temperature, wind, soil deficit[1], UVI, pressure, dry bulb temperature, wet bulb temperature, dew point temperature, and relative humidity. NIWA maintains several sites for measuring all these parameters all over Auckland except UVI.

---

[1] Soil moisture deficit, where full is 0 mm, and empty is 150 mm (AWC Available Water Capacity), refer National Climate Database: https://cliflo.niwa.co.nz/, for more details.

For recording UVI, there are only five sites all over NZ. For our research, the site closest to Auckland, the one at *Leigh Marine Observatory*, was chosen for acquiring data for this parameter.

Air Quality Data. The air quality monitoring program comprises two different types of parameters:

1. Particulate matter which includes $PM_{2.5}$, PM_{10}
2. Gaseous Pollutants consisting of *oxides of nitrogen, carbon monoxide, sulphur dioxide, ozone*

Air quality data was collected from eight different sites dispersed over the region of Auckland, and these sites are managed by Auckland Council. The parameters that were included under this category were: PM_{10}, $PM_{2.5}$, NO_X, NO_2, *Ozone, Black Carbon (880), Black Carbon (370)*, and SO_2. The number with black carbon corresponds to the wavelength at which black carbon is measured by the device called an aethalometer. Several parameters were reported at only one site, like readings for black carbon parameter were available at only one site, which was at Henderson (represented as Site 2 in Fig. ??). So this study does not signify the stratification related to spatial relevance.

Google Trends Data. Google data can be used to tell stories. There has been work done in the past [11] that demonstrates the linkage between *social media data and disease case data*. Google is the generic choice and the most visited website worldwide, so we explored *Google Trends* as a social media resource. This dataset allowed examination of the search trend, and data under this category was collected on a daily basis and refined by keywords related to asthma in the Auckland region. The keywords used for refinement were: *respiratory, lungs, asthma, cough, chronic, oxygen, bacteria, inhaler, wheezing, puffer, and asthma attack*. These trends data provide facts about how many searches related to asthma were performed each day in the Auckland region.

3.2 Data Preparation

The statistics forming the hospital data for asthma-related visits and admissions are in the form of aggregated daily values. The missing entries were filtered based on dates absent from the hospital admissions and ED visits data. They were subsequently allocated a zero value, assuming there were no asthma-related admissions or hospitalisations on those days. The data for meteorological factors were also aggregated 24-h values except for UVI, which were in the form of 10-min data readings. In contrast, most of the parameters under the air quality category were hourly values. The readings collected with frequency in minutes or hours were agglomerated to obtain the 24-h aggregated values accounting for continuous daily data. The Google Trends data were the daily search volume scaled and were comparable through time.

The aggregated value for every parameter, together with the date column, forms the respective dataset for every parameter, which is then cleaned from outliers. The outliers were detected using the *Inter-Quartile Range (IQR) proximity rule*. The outliers detected are treated by capping them within the 25th and 75th percentile range. The datasets corresponding to all the meteorological and air quality factors, plus the Google Trends, form the predictors for predicting the target variable: *asthma-related ED visits and hospitalisations.*

The next step involves handling missing values for the input variables; *missing values* is defined as the data values that are not present for some variables in the dataset. There can be different ways to fill these values, the methods chosen depend on why those missing values may have arisen. As already stated, missing values for hospital data might have been due to the absence of admissions on a day, whereas the missing values corresponding to input predictor variables may be because of device failure, human errors, and others and are therefore filled using the mean function.

The data values for all the parameters were acquired from different sources and spanned varying degrees of magnitude, range, and units. Therefore, each parameter was scaled to acquire a standard range. The method we have used in this research for scaling is *standardisation*. A variable is scaled by subtracting the mean (called centring) and dividing by the standard deviation to shift the distribution to have a mean of zero and a standard deviation of 1.

To convert this problem into classification, we classified ED and hospitalisation data related to asthma based on the standardised values into two categories; *High and Low*. *High* represents the days on which the number of patients was greater than the 70th percentile while the rest of the days were labelled as *Low*. Thus for this study, the 70th percentile was used as the threshold value.

3.3 Data Analysis and Feature Selection

To obtain clinical validation from the clinical advisor, an initial phase of data analysis was conducted to acquire contextual insights and ensure interpretability. Given that the majority of the prediction methods employed fell within the realm of classical machine learning models, a process of feature selection was carried out. An initial assessment was done to analyse the association between asthma-related ED visits and admissions data on one side and the predictor data on another side by using *Pearson's Correlation Coefficient or PCC*. To determine whether the correlation between the two variables is significant, the *p-value* obtained while calculating the correlation coefficient is compared to the significant level. Typically, a significant level expressed by α (alpha) equal to 0.05 is used. A *p-value* $\leqslant \alpha$ indicates that the correlation is statistically significant, while a *p-value* $> \alpha$ concludes that the correlation is not statistically significant.

The predictors witnessing significant correlation (according to *p-value*) with asthma-related ED visits and admissions were used as inputs for further processing. Changes in weather conditions or pollutants levels may not have an immediate impact on asthma conditions; instead, they may exacerbate asthma conditions leading to a delay between an environmental change and presentation to the ED or hospital. The values of these predictors on a particular day may not be linked with asthma-related ED visits and hospital admissions on the same day due to this delay. The lagged effect was applied to predictor variables to achieve the best representation between predictors and the target variable. The results in Table 2 below depict the result of the correlation calculation and analytical summary for all the parameters; the second and third column expresses the mean and standard deviation for the preprocessed data values for the respective parameter.

Table 2. Analytical summary of predictors.

Parameter	Mean	Std Dev	Correlation
Black Carbon (880)	2194.78	1873.76	0.1433
Black Carbon (370)	2788.81	2581.86	0.1348
Dew Point Temperature	12.09	3.75	−0.1184
Dry Bulb Temperature	15.51	3.88	−0.1642
NO_x	135.00	64.69	0.0962
NO_2	51.77	18.97	0.1734
Ozone	54.89	14.15	0.1788
$PM_{2.5}$	8.14	4.31	0.1008
PM_{10}	25.69	8.19	0.0326
Pressure	1016.05	7.69	−0.0154
Relative Humidity	80.90	11.44	0.1108
Soil Deficit	47.26	47.77	−0.1963
Temperature	18.45	3.65	−0.1923
Trends Data	67.82	39.39	0.1314
UVI	1.09	0.85	−0.1887
Wet Bulb Temperature	13.65	3.49	−0.1451
Wind	3.06	1.17	0.0731

The next step towards developing a predictive model was selecting the most crucial and relevant features from the vast list of features in a given dataset, thereby reducing the complexity of a model and making it easier to interpret. Basically, two methods were employed for feature selection: *forward feature selection and Extra Trees*. On the other hand, bagged decision trees, that is, Extra Trees, work by estimating the importance of features.

3.4   Prediction Model

Finally, the date and number of patients columns were dropped to obtain a pair representing the complete dataset in the form (X, y). Here, X represents the predictor variables and is a matrix of size (1097 × 14), while y is the class variable representing the number of asthma-related visits and hospitalisations either as Low or High. The ratio of samples for the Low to High class was 866 to 231. The numeric value used for class *Low* was *0* while for *High* was *1*. The complete dataset was divided into training and test sets in a ratio of 50:50.

The prediction modelling process was further divided into sub-phases according to three different methodologies used for prediction modelling, which are discussed below:

Method 1: **Using standard machine learning algorithms.**

In the first phase, four standard machine learning algorithms were executed to obtain the prediction model for asthma. These techniques were *MLP, RF, SVM, and XGB. MLP* is a feed-forward ANN model that is used for mapping a set of input variables to the appropriate output. An *RF* algorithm consists of many decision trees and produces the outcome based on the prediction of the decision trees. The final output is generated by taking the average or mean of the output from various trees. *SVM* is a fast and dependable classification algorithm that performs very well with a limited amount of data to analyse. *XGB* is a boosting algorithm that is based on gradient-boosted decision trees.

Method 2: **Using an ensemble by combining different algorithms.**

In the second phase, an ensemble classifier was developed by combining three classifiers as building blocks, as illustrated in Fig. 2. Thus, the three classifiers' predictions act as inputs into the ensemble, which produces the final prediction by employing the *majority voting* mechanism. Out of three, two classifiers were built using XGB classifier algorithms with distinctive parameter configurations. The reason for choosing XGB in this ensemble modelling will be explained in the next section. The third model, whose predictions were used in this ensemble, was obtained by applying Autoregressive Integrated Moving Average (ARIMA) algorithm. In order to check the usability of past hospitalisations data values for predicting future demands, the ARIMA model was chosen as the third input for the ensemble model. This algorithm is based on statistical analysis that utilises time series data values to understand the data patterns, and by using the past values, it produces future predictions. Here, the ARIMA classifier was trained using the past values of asthma-related hospitalisations. The input for the ARIMA model was the actual number of daily asthma-related hospitalisations instead of the target class. As a result, this model predicts future values for the number of asthma-related hospitalisations, which were then converted into suitable classes using the 70th percentile, as mentioned above.

Method 3: **Using standard machine learning algorithms on over-sampled dataset.**

The above-discussed methodologies *Method 1* and *Method 2* were implemented on the dataset where the number of instances under classes 0 and 1 were 866 and 231, respectively. Therefore, to obtain a fair, balanced classification scenario, over-sampling techniques were applied to generate synthetic data. Subsequently, two methodologies, SMOTE and random over-sampling, were utilised to obtain a balanced dataset concerning the above-specified classes, viz. 0 and 1. After obtaining a balanced dataset, an array of standard machine learning algorithms (MLP, RF, SVM, and XGB) listed in Method 1 were executed on this balanced dataset.

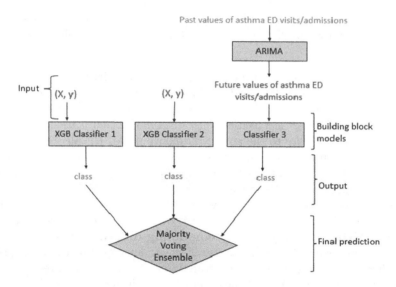

Fig. 2. Ensemble Modeling using three base models with final classification generated using majority voting mechanism.

4   Results

All experiments were performed on a 64-bit Windows running on a 4×3.40 GHz Intel Core i5 CPU with 16 GB of memory.

The results obtained after calculating the Pearson correlation coefficient have been analysed in Table 2. These results have been produced after applying the lagged effect. All the values for the coefficient were significant at the 0.01 level except SO2 which managed to achieve a correlation of 0.0628 with a p-value of 0.0377, so SO2 was removed from the list of predictors for further processing. From the results represented in this table, we could witness a small relationship between asthma-related visits and admissions with PM_{10}, Pressure, and NO_X. Even though the value of the correlation coefficient turned out to be small for these attributes but dropping them from the prediction model produced unfavourable consequences on accuracy. Therefore, these variables were included to develop the prediction model. Based upon the results of feature selection methods, three attributes were dropped from the predictor list, which was NO_2, Relative Humidity, and Dry Bulb Temperature, as these parameters seemed irrelevant to the model.

The execution of the prediction model listed under the three methodologies in the previous section has been assessed in terms of three different metrics;

Accuracy, Precision, and Recall. The performance of all the existing machine learning algorithms covered in the first methodology (viz MLP, RF, SVM, and XGB) have been demonstrated in Table 3. It can be seen out of four basic models, XGB Classifiers perform the best for all three measures. All the algorithms have comparable accuracy, but XGB classifiers outperformed with regard to precision.

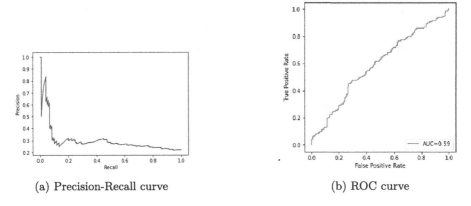

(a) Precision-Recall curve   (b) ROC curve

Fig. 3. a) Precision-Recall curve b) ROC curve for XGB classifier.

Besides this, two diagnostic tools that assist in interpreting the prediction of probabilities for binary classification problems are the Precision-Recall curve and the ROC curve. Figure 3 displays the Precision-Recall and ROC curve for the XBG classifier. AUC here specifies the area under the curve, which is another metric used for accessing the accuracy of a model. An excellent model tends to obtain an AUC close to 1, while a 0 value of AUC signifies a poor model.

The results obtained on implementing ensemble modelling, discussed as a second methodology for prediction modelling in the previous section, have also been presented in Table 3. This ensemble model was built using two XGB classifiers plus a classifier using output from the ARIMA model. The reason for choosing XGB classifiers was the best performance shown by them out of all the algorithms executed in the first phase. The majority ensemble witnessed better performance than all the models generated in phase one. This improvement is due to the competency of ensemble modelling to decrease the number of misclassifications and boost the accuracy of the classifier.

Table 3. Comparative analysis of different Machine Learning algorithms.

Model	Accuracy (%)	Precision (%)	Recall (%)
MLP	78.51	76.02	78.51
RF	78.14	72.32	78.14
SVM	78.14	61.06	78.14
XGB	78.87	79.81	78.87
Ensemble	79.05	80.44	79.05

Table 4. Comparison of performance achieved through implementing different algorithms over-sampled data.

Model	SMOTE			Random Over-Sampling		
	Accuracy	Precision	Recall	Accuracy	Precision	Recall
MLP	70.79	70.85	70.79	80.37	81.27	80.37
RF	78.87	78.87	78.87	86.37	86.45	86.37
SVM	75.87	83.72	75.87	91.00	92.37	91.00
XGB	73.44	73.48	73.44	81.76	82.17	81.76

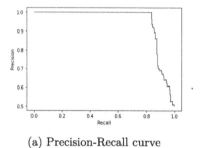

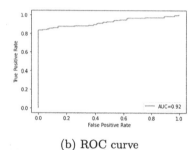

(a) Precision-Recall curve   (b) ROC curve

Fig. 4. a) Precision-Recall curve b) ROC curve for a balanced dataset using SVM.

The third modelling discussed in the third phase of prediction modelling in the previous section was dedicated to testing the over-sampling techniques. This section portrays the results obtained by over-sampling. As mentioned above, SMOTE and random over-sampling were used to generate data with the aim of acquiring a balanced dataset. With both of these techniques, the minority class, which is 1, was over-sampled to 866 instances, thus achieving equality for instances under both classes.

Table 4 presents the performance comparison between the two different balanced datasets generated by SMOTE and Random Over-Sampling. The results show that the model built on random over-sampled data performs superior to the data generated through SMOTE. Likewise, it can be noticed that SVM implemented on the random over-sampled data produces the best results out of all the methods discussed so far. Figure 4 shows the Precision-Recall and ROC curve for a balanced dataset using SVM. It can be noticed that the graphs here manifest superior model conduct than the performance depicted in Fig. 3 achieved through an unbalanced dataset.

5   Conclusion

The work discussed in this paper is the first study of its kind to explore population health prediction modelling in asthma, which has been a prominent health issue in NZ, providing an important foundation for future work. Under this study, we have explored different data sources and assessed their risk associated with asthma, thereby producing an accurate and precise prediction tool using a refined heterogeneous set of parameters originating from distributed sites. We have verified the feasibility of employing diverse machine learning approaches, encompassing both traditional machine learning and deep learning methods. Specifically, traditional machine learning models were favoured due to the constraints of small datasets and to get superior insights and interpretability in the development of prediction models. The maximum accuracy achieved in predicting asthma-related visits and admissions in Auckland is 91.00% with precision and recall holding values of 92.37% and 91.00%, respectively. We believe that this model has the potential to serve as a useful forecasting tool for health providers and organisations.

Exploration of analogous avenues can be undertaken by delving into alternative social media data sources such as Facebook, blogs, and similar platforms. Subsequent research endeavours could involve refining this model for various geographic regions and other non-communicable diseases like COPD and diabetes. It is important to note that the correlations between parameters and asthma conditions may diverge in distinct regions. Further progress can be directed toward assessing the performance of this model in prospective clinical studies involving real patient populations.

References

1. Accordini, S., et al.: The cost of persistent asthma in Europe: an international population-based study in adults. Int. Arch. Allergy Immunol. **160**, 93–101 (2012). https://doi.org/10.1159/000338998
2. Babin, S., et al.: Pediatric patient asthma-related emergency department visits and admissions in Washington, DC, from 2001–2004, and associations with air quality, socio-economic status and age group. Environ. Health Glob. Access Sci. Source **6**, 9 (2007). https://doi.org/10.1186/1476-069X-6-9
3. Bradley, S.: How common is asthma? Worldwide facts and statistics (2022). https://www.singlecare.com/blog/asthma-statistics/. Accessed 09 April 2022
4. Bridge, J., Blakey, J.D., Bonnett, L.J.: A systematic review of methodology used in the development of prediction models for future asthma exacerbation. BMC Med. Res. Methodol. **20** (2020)
5. Buyuktiryaki, B., et al.: Predicting hospitalization in children with acute asthma. J. Emergency Med. **44** (2013). https://doi.org/10.1016/j.jemermed.2012.10.015
6. Byers, N., Ritchey, M., Vaidyanathan, A., Brandt, A., Yip, F.: Short-term effects of ambient air pollutants on asthma-related emergency department visits in Indianapolis, Indiana, 2007–2011. J. Asthma Off. J. Assoc. Care Asthma **53**, 1–8 (2015). https://doi.org/10.3109/02770903.2015.1091006
7. Chawla, N., Bowyer, K., Hall, L., Kegelmeyer, W.: Smote: synthetic minority oversampling technique. J. Artif. Intell. Res. (JAIR) **16**, 321–357 (2002). https://doi.org/10.1613/jair.953
8. Custovic, A., et al.: Eaaci position statement on asthma exacerbations and severe asthma. Allergy **68**(12), 1520–1531 (2013). https://doi.org/10.1111/all.12275

9. Khatri, K., Tamil, L.: Early detection of peak demand days of chronic respiratory diseases emergency department visits using artificial neural networks. IEEE J. Biomedical Health Inform, 1 (2017). https://doi.org/10.1109/JBHI.2017.2698418
10. Kumar, B.: 10 Techniques to deal with Imbalanced Classes in Machine Learning (2020). https://www.analyticsvidhya.com/blog/2020/07/10-techniques-to-deal-with-class-imbalance-in-machine-learning/. Accessed 2 Oct 2021
11. Ram, S., Zhang, W., Williams, M., Pengetnze, Y.: Predicting asthma-related emergency department visits using big data. IEEE J. Biomedical Health Inform. **19** (2015). https://doi.org/10.1109/JBHI.2015.2404829
12. Soyiri, I., Reidpath, D.: An overview of health forecasting. Environ. Health Prevent. Med. **18** (2012). https://doi.org/10.1007/s12199-012-0294-6

Discovering Maximal High Utility Co-location Patterns from Spatial Data

Vanha Tran$^{(\boxtimes)}$ 🆔

FPT University, Hanoi 155514, Vietnam
`hatv14@fe.edu.vn`

Abstract. Compared with traditional prevalent co-location patterns (PCPs), high-utility co-location patterns (HUCPs), which consider the utility of spatial features and instances, can more effectively expose interesting relationships hidden in spatial data. However, just like traditional PCPs, there are too many redundant patterns in the mining results. Users are hard to understand and apply the results. Therefore, this work proposes a concise representation of the HUCP mining results, maximal high-utility co-location patterns. Maximal HUCPs can effectively reduce redundant patterns by designing a constraint of a HUCP with its supersets. The mining results become more concentrated and convenient for users to apply. Unfortunately, the common mining methods for maximal PCPs are not suitable for discovering maximal HUCPs since the downward closure property that is often utilized to reduce the candidate search space is not available in HUCP mining. Unnecessary candidates cannot be effectively pruned in advance. Thus, a new mining algorithm, which can effectively overcome the above problem, is proposed in this work. The algorithm first enumerates all maximal cliques of the input data set. Then it arranges these maximal cliques into a special hash map structure. After that, an upper bound of the candidate maximal patterns can be determined. The instances that participate in each candidate are quickly obtained from this hash structure. Finally, maximal HUCPs are filtered efficiently. The effectiveness and efficiency of the proposed method are demonstrated through synthetics and real data sets.

Keywords: Prevalent co-location pattern · Maximal high-utility co-location pattern · Downward closure property · Maximal clique

1 Introduction

Many areas such as business, geographic search logs, environmental science, and so on are daily generating large and rich spatial data sets. These data sets involve spatial information of the events that users are of interest. For example, Fig. 1 shows a typical spatial data set, i.e., a point of interest (POI) data set, that is collected from facility points of Beijing, China [10]. The spatial events (also call instances) are any points of interested facilities such as a bank of China outlet (A.1), a KFC (B.2), Shagou intersection west bus station (C.1),

© The Author(s), under exclusive license to Springer Nature Singapore Pte Ltd. 2023
S. Wu et al. (Eds.): PKAW 2023, LNAI 14317, pp. 15–28, 2023.
https://doi.org/10.1007/978-981-99-7855-7_2

and so on. These spatial instances are categorized into different types of interest called spatial features. Continuing with the previous example, the bank of China outlet and the industrial and commercial bank of China outlet are categorized into bank types (feature A). KFC and McDonald's are divided into fast food restaurant types (feature B). Shagou intersection west and Dongcui intersection bus stations are classified into bus station types (feature C). How to discover valuable knowledge from spatial data sets becomes an important task in data mining.

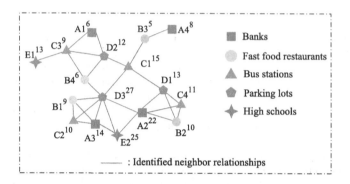

Fig. 1. A POI data set of Beijing, China.

A PCP is a group of spatial features whose instances frequently occur together in neighbourhood of each other [13]. PCPs have been proved to be an effective tool for discovering hidden and valuable relationships between spatial features in spatial data sets. For example, in a local-based service, based on a POI data set of Shanghai, China, we found that within a radius of 250 m, a group of shopping centers, fast foods, and parking lots appears together frequently [8]. Thus, {Shopping centers, Fast foods, Parking lots} is a PCP. This pattern can supply valuable information to different application domains. The information from this pattern can help you plan your trip. If you want to go shopping in a mall, there are parking lots in the neighboring area (within 250 m) of the mall to facilitate your parking. Then after shopping, you can grab a quick snack nearby. If you are a businessman who wants to find a location to set a new fast food restaurant, this PCP can provide you with a valuable reference. You should place your new fast food restaurant in the neighborhood (within a 250m radius) of shopping centers and parking lots. Taking advantage of the high customer flow rate of shopping centers and the convenience of parking lots, your store should have a good profit. This pattern can also serve as a reference for urban planners, i.e., where and how far should they arrange parking lots? PCPs have been widely used in many fields such as disease control [13], public health [6], transportation [7,11], social science [1,3], and so on.

However, in traditional PCPs, all features and instances are regarded as equally important. Only the prevalence of special spatial feature combinations is considered. For example, the importance of shopping centers and parking lots is equal, or the importance of two fast food restaurants is the same. But in fact, there is a big difference in the importance of shopping centers and parking lots, or the two fast food restaurants have different business concepts and other factors that lead to the income of the two restaurants being totally different. It is obvious that there is a big difference between spatial features and instances in space. If the factor is not considered, the traditional PCPs may not be able to fully reveal the valuable rules hidden in spatial data sets.

To take into account the differences that exist between spatial features and instances in co-location pattern mining, each instance is assigned a value to reflect its importance (called utility). For example, as shown in Fig. 1, the super-script of each instance indicates the utility value of that instance, e.g., A.1^6 means that the utility of A.1 is 6. We are interested in discovering those patterns from data whose utility is not smaller than a user-specified interesting threshold. These patterns are called high utility co-location patterns (HUCPs) [9].

However, there is the same problem as the traditional PCP mining, the mining results of HUCPs often contain too many patterns, especially when the user sets a low interesting threshold. This makes it difficult for users to understand, absorb and apply mining results. Therefore, a maximal HUCP concept is proposed in this work to realize a concise representation of the mining results. A pattern is called a maximal HUCP if its utility is not smaller than the user-specified interesting threshold and has no high utility supersets.

Unfortunately, the measurement scale in mining HUCPs does not satisfy the downward closure property [13]. That is, if a pattern is high utility, its super- or sub- sets may be or not be high. Thus, if we use the common level-wise generating-testing candidate mining framework [8,12,13] that is often used in discovering maximal PCPs, the mining efficiency will be extremely low since many unnecessary candidates cannot be effectively pruned in advance.

To address this problem, this work designs a top-down mining algorithm that is developed on maximal spatial instance cliques (any pairs of spatial instances in a maximal clique have a neighbor relationship) to enumerate all maximal HUCPs that meet the interesting threshold set by users.

The remainder of this paper is organized as follows: Sect. 2 briefly reviews the relevant definitions of HUCPs and gives the definition of maximal HUCPs. Section 3 describes the detail of the maximal spatial instance clique-based mining framework. Section 4 performs a series of experiments to demonstrate the effectiveness and efficiency of the proposed method. Section 5 summarizes the work of this paper and suggests future work.

2 Maximal High Utility Co-location Patterns

Given a spatial data set $S = \{I_1, ..., I_m\}$, where $I_t = \{f_t.i_1, ..., f_t.i_n\}$, $1 \leq t \leq m$ is the set of spatial instances that are categorized into feature type f_t, let $F = \{f_1, ..., f_m\}$ be a collection of feature types that the user is of interest. An spatial instance $f_t.i \in I_t$ is represented by a triple vector $\langle f_t, i, (x, y), u \rangle$, where i, (x, y), and u are the identification, the location of it in space, and its utility value that is assigned by users to reflect the importance of the instance, respectively. For convenience, the utility of an instance is referred to as $u(f_t.i) = u$.

If the distance between two instances that belong to different feature types is smaller than a distance threshold d given by users, i.e., $dist(f_t.i, f_h.j) \leq d$, the two instances have a neighbor relationship or they are neighbors. A set of all neighboring instances of an instance $f_t.i$ is defined as $NB(f_t.i) = \{f_h.j \mid dist(f_t.i, f_h.j) \leq d, \forall f_h.j \in S\}$.

Definition 1 (Spatial co-location pattern). A spatial co-location pattern c is a subset of the spatial feature set F and denoted as $c = \{f_1, ..., f_k\}$. The number of features in c is called the size of the pattern, i.e., c is a size k pattern.

Definition 2 (Row instance and table instance). Given $c = \{f_1, ..., f_k\}$, a row instance of c is a set of spatial instances that includes an instance of each feature in c and any pairs of them are satisfied the neighbor relationship. The set of all row instances of c is called its table instance and denoted as $T(c)$.

Definition 3 (Participating instance). The participating instances of a feature f_t in a co-location pattern $c = \{f_1, ..., f_k\}$ is the set of all instances of f_t that are in the table instances $T(c)$ and denoted as

$$PaI(f_t, c) = \{f_t.i \mid f_t.i \in T(c)\} \tag{1}$$

For example, as shown in Fig. 1, under a distance threshold d given by users to define a neighbor relationship, after materializing the neighbor relationship, these instances that satisfy the neighbor relationship are connected by a solid line. The neighboring instance set of each spatial instance is listed in Table 1.

Table 1. Neighboring instance sets.

A1	C3, D2	B3	A4, C1	D1	A2, B2, C1, D4
A2	B2, C4, D1, D3, E2	B4	C3, D2, D3	D2	A1, B4, C1
A3	B1, C2, D3, E2	C1	B3, D1, D2	D3	A2, A3, B1, B4, C1, C2, E2
A4	B3	C2	A3, B1, D3	E1	C3
B1	A3, C2, D3	C3	A1, B4, D2, E1	E2	A2, A3, D3
B2	A2, C4, D1	C4	A2, B2, D1		

We consider a pattern $c = \{A, C, D\}$. A row instance of c is $\{A2, C4, D1\}$. The table instance of c is $T(c) = \{\{A1, C3, D2\}, \{A2, C4, D1\}, \{A3, C2, D3\}\}$. The participating instances of the features in c are $PaI(A, c) = \{A1, A2, A3\}$, $PaI(C, c) = \{C2, C3, C4\}$, and $PaI(D, c) = \{D1, D2, D3\}$.

Definition 4 (Utility of a spatial feature). The utility of a spatial feature $f_t \in F$ is the sum of the utility of all instances that belong f_t and denoted as

$$u(f_t) = \sum_{f_t.i \in I_t} u(f_t.i) \tag{2}$$

Definition 5 (Utility of a feature in a co-location pattern). The utility of a spatial feature $f_t \in c = \{f_1, ..., f_k\}$ is the sum of the utility of the participating instances of f_t in c and denoted as

$$u(f_t, c) = \sum_{f_t.i \in PaI(f_t,c)} u(f_t.i) \tag{3}$$

For example, in Fig. 1, the utility of A is $u(A) = u(A1) + u(A2) + u(A3) + u(A4) = 6 + 22 + 14 + 8 = 50$. Similarly, the utility values of B, C, and D are 30, 45, 52, and 38, respectively. The utility of A in co-location pattern $c =\{$A, C, D$\}$ is $u(A, c) = u(A1) + u(A2) + u(A3) = 6 + 22 + 14 = 42$. With the same calculation, the utility values of C and D in c are 30 and 52, respectively.

Definition 6 (Intra-utility ratio). Given a co-location pattern $c = \{f_1, ..., f_k\}$, the intra-utility ratio of a feature $f_t \in c$ is the proportion of the utility of f_t in c to the utility of feature f_t and denoted as

$$IntraUR(f_t, c) = u(f_t, c)/u(f_t) \tag{4}$$

Definition 7 (Inter-utility ratio). The inter-utility ratio of a feature f_t in a pattern $c = \{f_1, ..., f_k\}$ reflects the influence of the feature on the other features in pattern c and is defined as

$$InterUR(f_t, c) = \sum_{f_h \in c, f_h \neq f_t} u(f_h, c)/ \sum_{f_h \in c, f_h \neq f_t} u(f_h) \tag{5}$$

Definition 8 (Utility participation ratio, UPR). The UPR of f_t in $c = \{f_1, ..., f_k\}$ is the weighted sum of its intra-utility ratio and its inter-utility ratio, i.e.,

$$UPR(f_t, c) = \alpha \times IntraUR(f_t, c) + \beta \times InterUR(f_t, c) \tag{6}$$

where α and β are the weighted value of the intra-utility ratio and inter-utility ratio assigned by users and they satisfy the conditions $0 \leq \alpha, \beta \leq 1, \alpha + \beta = 1$.

Definition 9 (Utility participation index, UPI). The UPI of $c = \{f_1, ..., f_k\}$ is defined as the minimum UPR among the all features in the pattern, i.e.,

$$UPI(c) = min_{f_t \in c}\{UPR(f_t, c)\} \tag{7}$$

Definition 10 (High utility co-location pattern). Given a pattern $c = \{f_1, ..., f_k\}$, if its utility participation index is not smaller than a user-specified interesting threshold μ, $UPI(c) \geq \mu$, c is a high utility co-location pattern.

For example, consider $c = \{A, C, D\}$, we can compute $IntraUR(A, c) = \frac{u(A,c)}{u(A} = \frac{u(A1)+u(A2)+u(A3)}{u(A} = 0.84$, $IntraUR(C, c) = 0.67$, and $IntraUR(D, c) = 1$. The inter-utility ratios of the features in c are $InterUR(A, c) = \frac{u(C,c)+u(D,c)}{u(C)+u(D)} = 0.845$, $InterUR(C, c) = 0.92$ and $InterUR(D, c) = 0.76$. If a user set the weight values of the intra- and inter- utility ratios in the pattern are 0.7 and 0.3, respectively. We can compute $UPR(A, c) = \alpha \times IntraUR(A, c) + \beta \times InterUR(A, c) = 0.7 \times 0.84 + 0.3 \times 0.845 = 0.84$. Similarly, we can calculate $UPR(C, c) = 0.74$ and $UPR(D, c) = 0.93$. A user set an interesting threshold $\mu = 0.5$, pattern $c = \{A, C, D\}$ is a HUCP since we have $UPI(c) = min\{0.84, 0.74, 0.93\} = 0.74 \geq \mu = 0.5$.

Lemma 1. *The UPI does not hold the downward closure property.*

Proof. Please refer to [9] for more details.

Definition 11 (Maximal high utility co-location pattern). Given a pattern $c = \{f_1, ..., f_k\}$, this pattern is a maximal high utility co-location pattern if c is a HUCP and c has no supersets that are HUCPs.

For example, with the data set shown in Fig. 1, a user set $\alpha = 0.7$, $\beta = 0.3$, and $\mu = 0.5$, The maximal HUCPs found are: $\{A, B, C, D\}$, $\{A, D, E\}$.

3   The Proposed Mining Algorithm

3.1   Collecting Participating Instances

Participating instances are collected from row instances. How to quickly find out the row instances becomes a key issue. A row instance is also a clique. If we can list all the maximal cliques, we can easily extract all row instances and collect participating instances of candidates from these maximal cliques.

Although enumerating maximal cliques is an NP-hard problem, there are many efficient algorithms [2,4,5]. Algorithm 1 describes the pseudocode of an efficient and commonly used for enumerating maximal cliques [5]. After materializing the neighbor relationship on S, we obtain an undirect graph $G(S, E)$, in which S is a set of vertices (all instances) and E is a set of edges that connect neighboring instances. For convenience of description, an instance in S is also denoted as o_t. P and X are the set of instances that has not been computed and the set of instances that has already been considered to add to R, respectively (Step 1). And R is a clique. All instances in S are sorted by the degeneracy (Step 2). When $P \cup X = \emptyset$, there are no more instances that can add into R to form a larger clique, thus R is a maximal clique (Steps 7–8). Otherwise, for each instance o_t in $P \setminus NB(o_j)$, Algorithm 1 makes a recursive call by adding o_t into R and restricting P and X to the neighbors of o_t (Steps 12). After that, o_t is removed from P and put into X (Steps 13–14).

However, Algorithm 1 cannot be directly applied to our scenario. Because when the data set is large and dense, the algorithm will be time-consuming and

---

Algorithm 1. Enumerating maximal cliques

    Input: $G(S, E), NB$
    Output: a set of maximal cliques, MCs
1: $P \leftarrow S, R \leftarrow \emptyset, X \leftarrow \emptyset$
2: **for** o_i in a degeneracy ordering $o_0, ..., o_n$ of $G(S, E)$ **do**
3:     $P \leftarrow NB(o_i) \cap \{o_{i+1}, ..., o_n\}$
4:     $X \leftarrow NB(o_i) \cap \{o_0, ..., o_{i-1}\}$
5:     BRONKERBOSCHPIVOT$(P, \{o_i\}, X)$

6: **BRONKERBOSCHPIVOT**(P, R, X)
7: **if** $P \cup X = \emptyset$ **then**
8:     MCs.add(R)
9: **else**
10:     choose a pivot instance $o_j \in P \cup X$ with $P \cap NB(o_j) = \max\limits_{o_t \in P \cup X} |P \cap NB(o_t)|$
11:     **for** $o_t \in P \setminus NB(o_j)$ **do**
12:         BRONKERBOSCHPIVOT$(P \cap NB(o_t), R \cup \{o_t\}, X \cap NB(o_t))$
13:         $P \leftarrow P \setminus \{o_t\}$
14:         $X \leftarrow X \cup \{o_t\}$

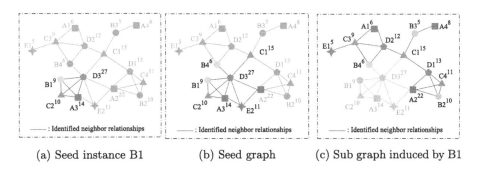

    (a) Seed instance B1   (b) Seed graph   (c) Sub graph induced by B1

Fig. 2. An illustration of the proposed graph partition approach.

consume a lot of memory. In order to improve the efficiency of enumerating maximal cliques, we design a graph partition approach. The entire data set is divided into several subgraphs, then Algorithm 1 is applied to these subgraphs.

Definition 12 (Seed instance and seed subgraph). Given an instance $f_t.i$, if the neighboring instance set of $f_t.i$ is not empty, $NB(f_t.i) \neq \emptyset$, $f_t.i$ is called a seed instance. The neighboring instance set of $f_t.i$ induces a seed subgraph, $G_{ind}(V_{ind}, E_{ind})$, where $V_{ind} = \{\{f_t.i\} \cup NB(f_t.i)\}$ and E_{ind} is the set of edges that connect neighboring instances in $NB(f_t.i)$.

Definition 13 (Subgraph induced by a seed instance). Given an instance $f_t.i$ and its seed subgraph $G_{ind}(V_{ind}, E_{ind})$, the subgraph is induced by the seed subgraph is defined as $G_{sub}(V_{sub}, V_{sub})$, where $V_{sub} = V_{ind} \cup NB(f_h.j), \forall f_h.j \in NB(f_t.i)$ and V_{ind} is the edges that connect all neighboring instances in V_{sub}.

For example, Fig. 2 illustrates the proposed graph partition approach when choosing B.1 as a seed instance. The subgraph induced by B1 is as in Fig. 2(b).

Then, we apply Algorithm 1 on the subgraph to list all maximal cliques. Finally, the seed subgraph is safely removed from S, as shown in Fig. 2(c).

Algorithm 2 describes the pseudocode for applying the proposed graph partition approach and utilizing Algorithm 1 to enumerate maximal cliques. Algorithm 2 first takes an instance as a seed instance, $f_t.i$ (Step 2) and then finds its subgraph G_{ind} (Step 3). Next the algorithm forms the subgraph of $f_t.i$, G_{sub} (Steps 5–7). The seed graph is deleted from S (Step 8). Finally, it employs Algorithm 1 to enumerate maximal cliques (Step 9).

Definition 14 (Participating instance hash table, PaITab). A PaITab is a two-level hash table structure, its keys are the sets of features in the maximal cliques and the values are a hash table in which the keys and values are the features of the instances and instance themselves in the maximal cliques.

Figure 3 shows the participating instance hash table that is constructed based on the maximal cliques enumerated from Fig. 1 by Algorithm 2.

Algorithm 2. Enumerating maximal cliques with the graph partition approach

Input: $G(S, E), NB$
Output: a set of maximal cliques, MC

1: **while** $S \neq \emptyset$ **do**
2:     $f_t.i \leftarrow S.\text{pop}()$
3:     $V_{ind}, E_{ind} \leftarrow \{f_t.i\} \cup NB(f_t.i))$
4:     $V_{sub}, E_{sub} \leftarrow V_{ind}, E_{ind}$
5:     **for** $f_h.j \in V_{ind}$ **do**
6:         $V_{sub} \leftarrow V_{sub} \cup NB(f_h.j)$
7:         $E_{sub} \leftarrow E_{sub} \cup NB(f_h.j)$
8:     $S.\text{remove}(V_{ind})$
9:     $MCs \leftarrow \text{Algorithm } 1(G_{sub}(V_{sub}, E_{sub}))$
10: **return** MCs

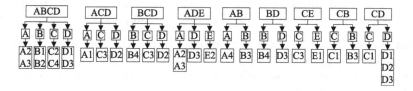

Fig. 3. The participating instance hash table constructed from Fig. 1.

3.2   Calculating Utility Participating Indexes

Algorithm 3 describes the pseudocode for constructing PaITab, computing the UPI of a pattern, and filtering maximal HUCPs, named MHUCPM. MHUCPM first takes all enumerated maximal cliques (executed in Algorithm 2) to construct the participating instance hash table (Steps 1–7). Then, it collects all keys of the hash table as candidates (Step 8). The largest size of the keys is the upper bound of the size of candidates and it is assigned for k (Step 9). After that, all size k candidates are processed. For each size k candidate c, if it is not a subset of any maximal HUCPs in the result set, we collect the participating instances of c from the hash table by gathering the values of all keys that are a superset of c and compute the utility participating index of c (Steps 12–17). If $UPI(c)$ is not smaller than the user-specified interesting threshold, c is a maximal HUCP (Steps 18–20). If not, the algorithm generates the direct subsets of c as new candidates and adds them into the candidate set $Cands$ (Steps 21). Finally, Algorithm 3 returns a set of maximal HUCPs (Step 22).

4   Experimental Results

4.1   Data Sets

There are two real data sets that are POI data sets extracted from Yelp data[1]. The utility of the instances of the two data sets is the number of check-ins on the instances. We also generate a set of synthetic data sets through a data generator [13]. Tables 2 and 3 list the main parameters of these data sets.

Algorithm 3. The proposed maximal HUCP mining algorithm, MHUCPM

Input: $G, NB, \mu, \alpha, \beta$
Output: a set of maximal HUCPs, $MHUCPs$

1: $MCs \leftarrow$ Algorithm 2
2: **for** $mc \in MCs$ **do**
3:      $key \leftarrow getFeatureSet(mc)$
4:      **if** $key \in PaITab$ **then**
5:          $PaITab.$update(mc)
6:      **else**
7:          $PaITab.$insert(mc)
8: $Cands \leftarrow$ getAllKeys$(PaITab)$
9: $k \leftarrow$ getMaximalSizeOfKey$(Cands)$
10: **while** $Cands$ is not $\emptyset$ **do**
11:      $SizekCands \leftarrow$ getAllSizekCands$(Cands, k)$
12:      **for** $c \in SizekCands$ **do**
13:          **if** c is not a subset of any patterns in $MHUCPs$ **then**
14:              **for** $key \in PaITab$ **do**
15:                  **if** $c \subseteq key$ **then**
16:                      $PaI(c) \leftarrow$ getParticipatingInstance()
17:              $UPI(c) \leftarrow$ computeUPI(PaI, α, β)
18:              **if** $UPI(c) \leq \mu$ **then**
19:                  $MHUCPs.$add(c)
20:              **else**
21:                  Generate direct subsets of c and add into $Cands$
22: **return** $MHUCPs$

---

[1] https://www.yelp.com/dataset.

Table 2. The main parameters of the real data sets.

Name	Area (m × m)	# features	# instances
Las Vegas	38,650 × 62,985	21	23,407
Toronto	23,416 × 56,035	20	17,128

Table 3. The main parameters of the synthetic data sets.

Figure	Area	# features	# instances
Figs. 4(a), 5(a), 6(a), 7(a), 8(a)	5K × 5K	15	50K
Fig. 9	5K × 5K	15	*

1K = 1000, * : variable

We choose the algorithm proposed by Wang et al. [9] as the comparison algorithm. This algorithm employs the level-wise generating-testing candidate mining framework to discover all HUCPs. Two maximal pattern mining algorithms, MaxColoc [12] and SGCT [10] are also chosen. Although these two are used to mine maximal PCPs and their measurement scale satisfies the downward closure property, the algorithm proposed in this paper can give better performance on dense and large data sets. All these algorithms are coded by C++ and performed on Intel(R) Core i7-3770 and 16 GB main memory of a computer.

4.2   Performance on Reducing Number of HUCPs

Figure 4 depicts all HUCPs and maximal HUCPs mined under different user-specified interesting thresholds on synthetic and real data sets. It can be seen that the maximal can effectively reduce the number of HUCPs. The lower the user-specified interesting threshold, the more HUCPs are discovered, the stronger the reducing ability of the maximal patterns.

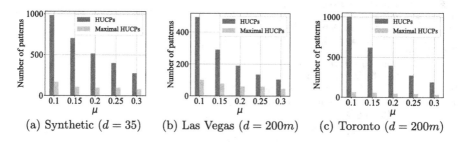

(a) Synthetic ($d = 35$)   (b) Las Vegas ($d = 200m$)   (c) Toronto ($d = 200m$)

Fig. 4. The comparison of numbers of HUCPs and maximal HUCPs ($mu = 0.2$).

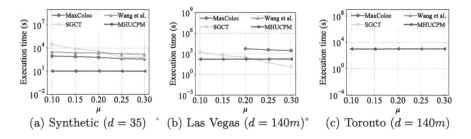

(a) Synthetic ($d = 35$)   (b) Las Vegas ($d = 140m$)   (c) Toronto ($d = 140m$)

Fig. 5. The execution time of the compared algorithms on different μ.

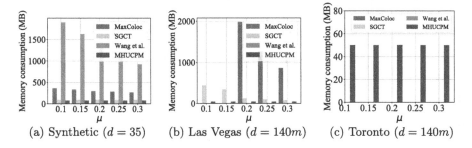

(a) Synthetic ($d = 35$)   (b) Las Vegas ($d = 140m$)   (c) Toronto ($d = 140m$)

Fig. 6. The memory consumption of the compared algorithms on different μ.

4.3   Performance on Different User-Specified Interesting Thresholds

Figures 5 and 6 depict the execution time and memory consumption of the compared algorithms on different μ values, respectively. As can be seen that at small values of μ, the performance of the three algorithms that employ the level-wise generating-testing candidate mining framework deteriorates rapidly. On the contrary, the proposed algorithm can provide efficient mining performance. There is a small change in the execution time and memory consumption of our algorithm when changing μ. Because when the threshold is set to different values, our algorithm only needs to query for the participating instances of candidates from the hash structure, without any other additional operations.

4.4   Performance on Different Distance Thresholds

Figures 7 and 8 show the execution time and memory consumption of the compared algorithms at different distance thresholds. It can be seen that as d increases, the execution time and memory consumption of each algorithm increase accordingly. But the performance of the three algorithms is degraded very quickly when the distance threshold increases. On the contrary, the algorithm we designed can give better performance. As the distance threshold increases, the execution time and memory consumption of the proposed algorithm increase correspondingly, but at a lower rate of increase.

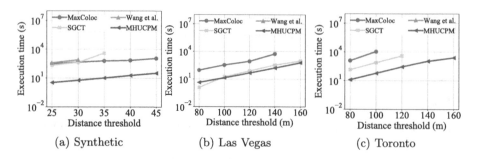

Fig. 7. The execution time on different distance thresholds ($\mu = 0.2$).

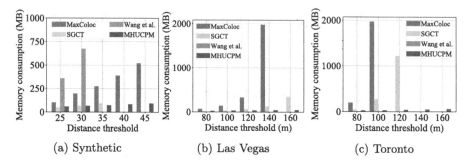

Fig. 8. The memory consumption on different distance thresholds ($\mu = 0.2$).

4.5 Performance on Different Numbers of Instances

As shown in Fig. 9, as the data set increases, the execution time and memory consumption of all algorithms increase accordingly. But the performance of the three algorithms drops sharply. For example, when the number of instances is larger than 160K, the three algorithms take too much time to complete the mining task. On the contrary, the proposed algorithm gives better performance and shows good scalability under large data sets.

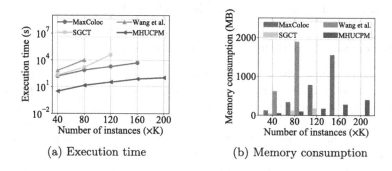

Fig. 9. The performance on different numbers of instances ($\mu = 0.2, d = 25$).

5   Conclusion

In this work, we propose a concise representation of HUCPs called maximal HUCPs. We also design an efficient algorithm to discover maximal HUCPs. Different from the traditional level-wise generating-testing candidate mining framework that relies heavily on the downward closure property of the measurement scale for pruning unnecessary candidates in advance to improve mining efficiency, the proposed algorithm can find out the upper bound of sizes of candidates and quickly collect participating instances that support these candidates through a query mechanic. We conduct experiments on both synthetic and real data sets. Experimental results prove that the proposed method can effectively reduce the number of HUCPs and give higher mining efficiency than the existing algorithms.

It is easy to find that based on the proposed graph partitioning approach, enumerating maximal cliques can be performed independently and simultaneously on each subgraph. Therefore, to further improve the performance of the proposed algorithm, our next work is to parallelize the algorithm.

References

1. Cai, J., Liu, Q., Deng, M., Tang, J.: Adaptive detection of statistically significant regional spatial co-location patterns. Comput. Environ. Urban **68**, 53–63 (2018)
2. Cheng, J., Zhu, L., Ke, Y., Chu, S.: Fast algorithms for maximal clique enumeration with limited memory. In: ACM SIGKDD, pp. 1240–1248 (2012)
3. Deng, M., Cai, J., Liu, Q., He, Z., Tang, J.: Multi-level method for discovery of regional co-location patterns. Int. J. Geogr. Inf. Sci. **31**(9), 1846–1870 (2017)
4. Eppstein, D., Löffler, M., Strash, D.: Listing all maximal cliques in sparse graphs in near-optimal time. In: Cheong, O., Chwa, K.-Y., Park, K. (eds.) ISAAC 2010. LNCS, vol. 6506, pp. 403–414. Springer, Heidelberg (2010). https://doi.org/10.1007/978-3-642-17517-6_36
5. Eppstein, D., Löffler, M., Strash, D.: Listing all maximal cliques in large sparse real-world graphs. Journal of Experimental Algorithmics **18**, 3–1 (2013)
6. Lei, L., Wang, L., Zeng, Y., Zeng, L.: Discovering high influence co-location patterns from spatial data sets. In: ICBK, pp. 137–144. IEEE (2019)
7. Liu, W., Liu, Q., Deng, M., Cai, J., Yang, J.: Discovery of statistically significant regional co-location patterns on urban road networks. Int. J. Geogr. Inf. Sci. **36**(4), 749–772 (2022)
8. Tran, V., Wang, L., Chen, H., Xiao, Q.: MCHT: a maximal clique and hash table-based maximal prevalent co-location pattern mining algorithm. Expert Syst. Appl. **175**, 114830 (2021)
9. Wang, L., Jiang, W., Chen, H., Fang, Y.: Efficiently mining high utility co-location patterns from spatial data sets with instance-specific utilities. In: Candan, S., Chen, L., Pedersen, T.B., Chang, L., Hua, W. (eds.) DASFAA 2017. LNCS, vol. 10178, pp. 458–474. Springer, Cham (2017). https://doi.org/10.1007/978-3-319-55699-4_28
10. Yao, X., Peng, L., Yang, L., Chi, T.: A fast space-saving algorithm for maximal co-location pattern mining. Expert Syst. Appl. **63**, 310–323 (2016)
11. Yao, X., Wang, D., Chen, L., Cui, S., Chi, T.: A spatial co-location mining algorithm based on a spatial continuous field with refined road-network constraints. In: IGARSS, pp. 5049–5052. IEEE (2018)

12. Yoo, J.S., Bow, M.: A framework for generating condensed co-location sets from spatial databases. Intell. Data Anal. **23**(2), 333–355 (2019)
13. Yoo, J.S., Shekhar, S.: A joinless approach for mining spatial colocation patterns. IEEE Trans. Knowl. Data Eng. **18**(10), 1323–1337 (2006)

Exploring the Potential of Image Overlay in Self-supervised Learning: A Study on SimSiam Networks and Strategies for Preventing Model Collapse

Li Xiao[1], Weihua Li[1(✉)], Quan Bai[2], and Minh Nguyen[1]

[1] Auckland University of Technology, Auckland, New Zealand
{li.xiao,weihua.li,minh.nguyen}@aut.ac.nz
[2] University of Tasmania, Hobart, Australia
Quan.Bai@utas.edu.au

Abstract. Self-supervised representation learning (SSL) has rapidly become a compelling avenue of research in visual tasks. Its performance, comparable to that of supervised learning, combined with its ability to mimic human perception, makes it an attractive area of study. The inherent simplicity of SSL also makes it easily accessible. However, data augmentation and collapse avoidance remain significant challenges. To address these issues, we have explored the use of image overlay in combination with principal Convolutional Neural Network models and an efficient SimSiam network. Our investigation led to three main findings. Firstly, while image overlay did not perform as efficiently as existing optimized augmentation methods, it showed potential to enhance the effectiveness of SSL tasks. Secondly, our research underscored the critical roles of data volume and augmentation in preventing a model collapse in SSL. This stands in contrast to pre-trained supervised learning, which places more emphasis on input image resolution and model size. Finally, our results indicated stability in the loss function within SSL, hinting at its potential to refine the model training process and encouraging the exploration of innovative augmentation methods. These empirical insights could be instrumental in simplifying and democratising deep learning techniques, making them more accessible and appealing to a broader audience. These findings will stimulate further research in this domain and contribute to the ongoing evolution of deep learning.

Keywords: Self-supervised learning · Image overlay · Data augmentation · SimSiam network

1 Introduction

Self-supervised representation learning (SSL) has emerged as a significant framework in machine learning [2,5,6]. It leverages the intrinsic structure and information in unlabeled data to extract valuable features without the need for explicit

S. Wu et al. (Eds.): PKAW 2023, LNAI 14317, pp. 29–42, 2023.
https://doi.org/10.1007/978-981-99-7855-7_3

human annotation. Among the various SSL approaches, Contrastive Learning (CL) has earned recognition for its effectiveness in discerning representations by contrasting similar and dissimilar pairs of data instances [5]. This technique has proven to be highly effective, not only in Natural Language Processing (NLP) but also across a broad spectrum of Computer Vision (CV) tasks [12].

High-performance SSL models have been developed in the domain of CV, which remarkably achieve strong results without heavily relying on labels or, in some cases, with very limited labelling. Additionally, methods that reduce computational and resource demands while retaining high performance have gained traction. Exemplary models like SimCLR [5] and SimSiam [6] have made significant steps in this direction. Despite these advances, dimensional or feature collapse poses a significant challenge to representation learning.

Dimensional collapse [11] is a phenomenon where the model fails to learn the essential, diverse features from the dataset and instead converges to a single point or a set of similar points in the feature space, irrespective of the input. This issue leads to a consistently low or even diminishing accuracy in downstream tasks, impeding the model's effectiveness in real-world scenarios. It is essentially a manifestation of overfitting within SSL, where the model is too focused on specific features in the training data and fails to generalise to unseen data. Our research aims to address this issue by exploring the application of image overlay and extension of image augmentation as potential strategies to prevent dimensional collapse. This approach is encouraged by recent SSL models like SimSiam, which stress the importance of feature diversity and redundancy reduction as a pathway to tackle this issue.

In this paper, we delve deep into the shortcomings of SSL models and propose enhancements. Firstly, we analyse SSL downstream tasks and discover a deficiency in accuracy compared to high-performance supervised tasks. This discrepancy is primarily attributable to the model's limitations or the data quality. To bridge this gap, we employ an extended data size with augmentation, thus driving performance improvement. Secondly, we conduct collapse experiments to identify potential model inadequacies. Instances of noticeable decline or stagnation in training performance indicate a misfit or over-complexity of the model in relation to the underlying patterns and structures in the data. Thirdly, we highlight the trade-offs involved in using larger datasets. Despite leading to faster convergence during training, the increased training time and resource consumption are notable drawbacks. We explore the use of image overlay techniques as a solution to this problem. These techniques optimise the training resources, enhancing efficiency and reducing memory usage. Next, we address the limitation of SSL models' generalisability to diverse large datasets. Despite their high performance, these models often fail to generalise across varied datasets. By applying a combination of image augmentation and overlay techniques, we enhance the model's performance on different datasets, thereby boosting its adaptability and generalisability. Finally, we turn our attention to the representation learning experiments, where minimal changes in the loss value are observed. This suggests an ineffective optimisation of the loss function. To address this, we propose the potential for advancements in unsupervised representation learning methods. We aim to improve the loss function's ability to capture critical features and patterns in the data.

2   Related Work

SSL has witnessed remarkable advances in recent years, with models such as Sim-CLR and SimSiam making significant contributions to the field. In this section, we review these models, delving into their architectural strategies, respective approaches to data augmentation, and model simplification. We also explore the prevalent issue of dimensional collapse in SSL models and discuss various viewpoints and strategies aimed at resolving this challenge.

2.1   Noteworthy Models

SimCLR, a pivotal SSL model, employs CL and a Siamese architecture to learn meaningful feature representations. Notably, it attains a top-1 accuracy of 95.3% on the CIFAR-10 dataset, which parallels the performance of a supervised ResNet-50 model [5]. This achievement owes itself to effectively incorporating diverse data augmentation techniques, resulting in a robust model with superior generalisation capabilities. However, the heavy computational requirements of SimCLR's original experiment pose a challenge to researchers with limited resources. To make their strategies more accessible, we adapt and incorporate data augmentation methods based on their work. It ranks 7×8 types of data augmentation methods combination and builds a foundation for future data argumentation work in this field.

SimSiam or Simple Siamese network, an innovative SSL model, boasts a simpler architecture than its predecessors while maintaining competitive performance [6]. It diverges from SimCLR by removing the negative sample from the contrastive loss function and introducing a stop-gradient operation for better training efficiency. This simplification enables SimSiam to achieve comparable results with fewer resources, eliminating the need for extensive batch sizes with improved data augmentation methods set from SimCLR and MoCo [8]. Although it may be challenging to reproduce the exact results due to variations in experimental settings, we aim to achieve comparable performance within a shorter training period of 100 epochs.

2.2   Mitigating Dimensional Collapse

The phenomenon of dimensional collapse presents a significant obstacle in SSL, which several studies have sought to understand and overcome [13,15,20]. Because the representation learning did not use labels, it often uses labelled data to evaluate the model in downstream tasks by simple and robust classifiers like k-Nearest neighbours and collapse only happens in the representation learning phase. Researchers have tried many methods to mitigate dimensional collapse such as data augmentation [16,17] and instance repetition [10] and clusters method [1,3] etc. Investigations into SimSiam, a non-contrastive SSL method, have revealed that it is particularly susceptible to collapse when the model's capacity is insufficient relative to the size of the dataset. Several strategies have been proposed to address this issue, including continual and multi-epoch training, which can significantly improve the model's performance [15].

Most mitigating dimensional collapse methods focus on model updating the Siamese architecture [7] or integrating methods into the core process like cluster [3] etc. Meanwhile, because the self/unsupervised contains no label, it is natural to think about the data attributes like augmentation and size and also image overlay. Image overlay or image fusion is a common method used, mostly as an image augmentation method and combines different sources. For instance, research [18] overlays infrared and visible images for the image process. In the medical image industry, image overlay has been widely used [21]. However, there are not many improvements in supervised learning, it also can be found in our supervised learning experiment. As common sense information in another image can be covered and changed, but in the SSL task we rely on the change. Especially, a Siamese network like SimSiam without negative pairs. This means image overlay could be a different data augmentation method. Theoretically, image overlay not only can enhance the features of target images but also reduce the data size, which is efficient in SSL.

3   Research Design

This research is structured around experimental investigations and comparisons of three distinct models: supervised learning with transfer learning, SSL via SimSiam, and the integration of overlays with both models. These experiments are performed on a single GPU (A6000) with 100 epochs on the CIFAR-10 dataset [14]. Each epoch is followed by an evaluation of the test set. These experiments aim to assess and compare the potential performance of the different models in encoding images.

3.1   Supervised Learning Design

We first establish a baseline by training two pre-existing models, ResNet-18 and ResNet-50 [9], on the CIFAR-10 dataset. Our supervised learning experiments comprise two stages: transfer learning and fine-tuning. We use transfer learning to exploit the pre-trained models' capabilities, followed by fine-tuning to optimize performance for the CIFAR-10 dataset. We adjust various hyperparameters such as optimizer types, learning rate, weight decay, image size, kernel size for the first convolution layer, and batch size to optimize the setup for our environment.

Transfer Learning Stage. To exploit the strengths of the pre-existing ResNet models, we replace the fully connected (FC) layer with a new linear layer for the CIFAR-10 dataset. Initially, we only allow the parameters of the FC layer to be trainable, effectively freezing the rest. We train the model with the Adam optimizer, setting the learning rate to 0.001 and weight decay to 10^{-4} for 10 epochs [7,19].

Fine-Tuning Stage. Following the transfer learning stage, we unlock all parameters of the trained model for fine-tuning. The Stochastic Gradient Descent (SGD) optimiser is applied, with a learning rate of 0.01, momentum of 0.9, and weight decay of 10^{-4}. This fine-tuning process is carried out for 90 epochs. The training progress is tracked using loss and accuracy metrics, and the best model, as determined by validation accuracy, is saved.

3.2 SSL Experiment Design

Our SSL experiment predominantly revolves around SimSiam, incorporating the publicly available data and insights from the original paper. We structure our experiment into representation learning and a downstream task utilising the K-Nearest Neighbors (KNN) algorithm instead of Fully Connected Neural Network (FCNN) on the trade-off between computational efficiency and the capacity to capture complex representation patterns [4]. This structure enables us to accurately assess the performance of our SimSiam model.

As can be seen from Fig. 1, the representation learning phase serves as the cornerstone of our experiment. The extend and overlay are two different strategies before augmentations. A scheduler initiates this process, initialising the SimSiam model and the corresponding training loop by encoder, projector and predictor with the cross symbol of stop gradient. Simultaneously, it adjusts the model's foundational architecture, hyper-parameters, and optimisation method. Furthermore, the scheduler implements the loss criterion and stop gradient operation, as denoted by Eqs. 1 and 2, respectively. Each epoch of the 100-epoch training loop adapts the learning rate and weight decay according to the SimSiam conventions, leading to a robust training regimen.

Key to our research design is the assimilation of three foundational aspects from SimSiam: the Similarity Loss function, the Stop Gradient concept, and the SGD optimiser [6].

$$\mathcal{L}_{\text{SimSiam}} = -\frac{1}{2}\left(\frac{p_1 \cdot z_2}{\|p_1\|_2 \cdot \|z_2\|_2} + \frac{p_2 \cdot z_1}{\|p_2\|_2 \cdot \|z_1\|_2}\right) \tag{1}$$

The Eq. 1 represents the loss function $\mathcal{L}_{\text{SimSiam}}$ used in the SimSiam framework [6]. It calculates the similarity between pairs of projected vectors p_1 and p_2 with target vectors z_2 and z_1, respectively. The loss is computed by taking the dot product between the projected vector p_1 and the target vector z_2, divided by the product of their magnitudes $\|p_1\|_2 \cdot \|z_2\|_2$. Similarly, the dot product between p_2 and z_1 is divided by the product of their magnitudes $\|p_2\|_2 \cdot \|z_1\|_2$. The two terms are then summed and divided by 2 and finally negated. This similarity loss function is commonly used in SSL tasks, where the objective is to maximise the similarity between augmented views of the same image while minimising the similarity between views of different images.

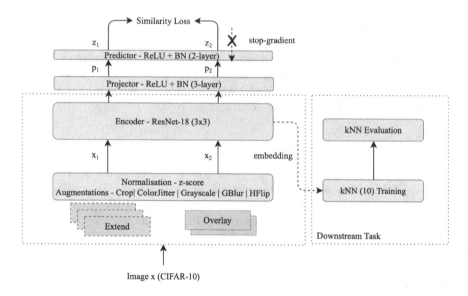

Fig. 1. Contrastive Learning process design.

The Stop Gradient concept is used in deep learning to prevent gradients from flowing backwards beyond a certain point during back-propagation. By applying a Stop Gradient operation or marking certain variables or layers, the gradients are not computed or used for parameter updates beyond that point. This technique is useful for freezing layers, preventing updates to specific parameters, handling adversarial attacks, or managing complex computational graphs where gradient reuse is necessary.

$$v_{t+1} = \mu \cdot v_t - \eta \cdot \text{stop\_gradient}(\nabla J(\theta_t, x_i, y_i)) - \lambda \cdot \eta \cdot \theta_t \qquad (2)$$

Equation 2 represents the stop gradient operation and v_{t+1} and v_t represent velocity or momentum in optimization, μ is a hyperparameter representing the momentum coefficient, η is the learning rate, λ is the weight decay. And most importantly the stop_gradient, which ensures that the gradient from loss function $\nabla J(\theta_t, x_i, y_i)$ does not affect the back-propagation. This means that the gradient does not flow through the stop gradient operation or impact the parameter update.

In our implementation, we made adjustments to the SGD optimizer by specifying certain hyper-parameters. Firstly, we set the learning rate to 0.025, which was obtained by multiplying 0.05 with the ratio of the batch size (128) to 256. This choice allowed us to appropriately adapt the learning rate based on the batch size employed. Additionally, we set the momentum factor to 0.9, which introduced inertia to the optimisation process. This factor helped in stabilising and accelerating convergence during training. Furthermore, we incorporated a weight decay factor of 10^{-4}. This factor served to discourage the proliferation of large weights within the model. By penalising overly complex representations, the weight decay factor promoted generalisation, thereby enhancing the model's ability to perform well on unseen data. By configuring the SGD optimizer with these specific hyper-parameters, our objective was to ensure effective parameter updates during training. This, in turn, improved the convergence and generalisation performance of the SimSiam model.

Another crucial aspect of SSL is data augmentation. In our approach, we utilise the data augmentation approach that is presented in the SimSiam paper, as shown in Table 1. These augmentation techniques are employed to enrich and diversify the training datasets, thereby enhancing the learning process.

Table 1. Data augmentation methods detailed in the SimSiam network.

Method	Description	Probability	Other Parameters
ResizedCrop	Crops and resizes the image	100%	padding=4
ColorJitter	Adjusts the color of the image	80%	BCSH = (0.4, 0.4, 0.4, 0.1)
Grayscale	Converts the image to grayscale	50%	N/A
Gaussian Blur	Apply Gaussian blur	20%	sigma = [.1, 2.]
HorizontalFlip	Flips the image horizontally	50%	N/A

The SimSiam model is primarily designed for SSL, aiming to extract substantial representations from unlabeled data. The model comprises three integral networks: the encoder, projector, and predictor. We have made some adjustments to the existing SimSiam model. The encoder, which is based on the ResNet-18 architecture, extracts image features. The projector network, incorporating three linear layers with batch normalisation and ReLU activation, transforms these features to enhance their relevance. The predictor network, a two-layer linear arrangement also with batch normalisation and ReLU activation, makes predictions based on the projected features. The forward method enables computations and returns the predictor outputs and intermediate feature embeddings, with downstream evaluation assessing their quality.

The downstream task in this context pertains to evaluating the trained model's performance on a classification task. As stated in the SimSiam paper but absent from their code, this task is performed using the K-Nearest Neighbors ($k = 10$) algorithm. We've developed the training and evaluation steps for this classifier utilising scikit-learn's KNeighborsClassifier. The training data is converted into a 2048-dimensional embedding vector and trained across 10 categories. Following this, the evaluation step calculates the top-1 accuracy using the test data. The resultant accuracy from this downstream task is an indicator of the model's performance and validates the effectiveness of the SSL model in generating meaningful feature representations applicable to classification tasks.

3.3 Overlay and Extend Adjustments

In our experiment, we evaluated the impact of overlays by incorporating randomly generated positive pairs into the dataset. These pairs, created through the application of two different augmentations to an input image, provided two augmented versions of the same image, ideal for CL. Introducing overlay pairs inevitably reduced the total dataset size. To rectify this, we implemented an extension adjustment, whereby our data size was initially reduced to 0.5 and then incremented relative to the scenario without overlays. This balanced the dataset size and ensured a reliable and accurate evaluation of the overlays' influence.

4 Findings and Discussions

Our experimental iterations have yielded results, including the evolution of training loss and evaluation accuracy. These outcomes, documented meticulously through figures and tables, are dissected in the ensuing sections. We focus our discussion on three central themes: the supervised benchmark, SSL collapse, and overlay comparison, hoping that our analytical insights significantly contribute to a better understanding of our approach's efficacy and performance.

4.1 Supervised Benchmark

Our supervised transfer learning results on the CIFAR-10 dataset provide a benchmark for comparison. Shown in Fig. 2, we achieved remarkable Top 1 accuracies of 97.55% and 95.71% using ResNet-50 and ResNet-18, respectively, displaying robust performance despite constrained computational resources. With increasing training epochs, we observed a consistent decrease in loss value and a rapid accuracy boost at the outset, particularly noticeable when the entire model was set to fine-tune.

Remarkably, only when the image size was set to 224×224 did we achieve 95% accuracy within 100 epochs, irrespective of the use of ResNet-50 or ResNet-18 [9]. This finding prompts us to question whether the exceptional performance is due to the pre-trained model being tailored to a 224×224 resolution or if the model intrinsically learns more efficiently when handling 224×224-sized images as opposed to the original 32×32 size. These insights act as a reference point for comparison with the ensuing SSL outcomes, enhancing our comprehension of model performance across different training methodologies.

4.2 Collapse in SimSiam

Figure 3 displays our observations from the SimSiam experiment where we tracked the progression of similarity loss and downstream task evaluations over six diverse trials. We noted distinct effects due to alterations in image size and the initial convolution kernel size, diverging from previous supervised learning results. Interestingly, the CIFAR-10 performance of most ResNet-50 encoder models was inferior to that of the ResNet-18 encoder, especially when an unsuitable combination of image size and convolution kernel size was used, such as pairing a 32×32 image with a 7×7 kernel.

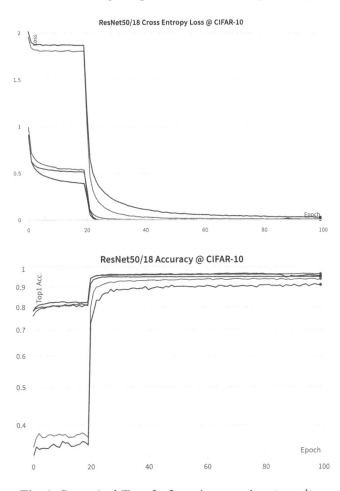

Fig. 2. Supervised Transfer Learning experiment results.

Table 2. ResNet-50 ACC. @CIFAR10: Overlay and Augment with Varying Data Size.

Methods @data	original	*1/2	*1	*2	*3	*5	*8
Overlay first @test	97.55%	91.90%	92.62%	92.37%	92.35%	91.81%	92.21%
Augment first @test	97.55%	93.70%	93.70%	93.91%	93.98%	93.74%	93.90%
Overlay first @training	99.99%	92.46%	92.49%	92.45%	92.57%	92.16%	92.27%
Augment first @training	99.99%	93.68%	93.89%	93.92%	93.73%	93.91%	93.66%

Despite utilising hyper-parameters consistent with SimSiam, discerning an optimal combination remained elusive. Certain configurations failed to demonstrate effective learning, as indicated by a lack of improved evaluation accuracy even after 30 training epochs. Furthermore, changes in similarity loss were less pronounced compared to supervised learning. Among all the configurations, only the combination of the ResNet-18 encoder with the original 32×32 image reso-

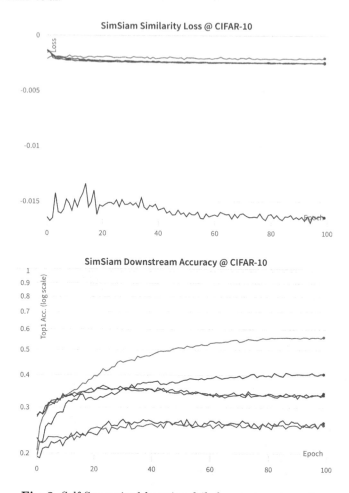

Fig. 3. Self-Supervised learning failed experiment results.

lution and a 3×3 convolution kernel yielded satisfactory outcomes. These experiments shed light on some intriguing patterns, including the quest for methods that might further improve accuracy performance.

4.3   Overlay Potential

Our experiments indicated that SSL often benefits more from complex data compared to unaltered data, in line with SimCLR's findings [5]. In this context, data augmentation holds a more crucial role in SSL than in supervised training (Fig. 4).

Due to distinct performance metrics and training strategies between SSL and supervised learning, Table 2 has been provided to delineate the best-retrained model results, with a focus on the overlay and extended-size augmentation dataset. These results exhibit a reduction in accuracy for both the test dataset

Fig. 4. A batch(100) of test images in augment and overlay.

and training data after augmentation and overlay application, although accuracy remains around 92–93%. This suggests that augmentation and overlay order do not substantially impact generalisation performance.

Under certain conditions, overlay techniques could potentially reduce the training dataset and expedite the learning process. Finally, as illustrated in Fig. 5, we collated training losses and downstream evaluation accuracy from the SimSiam experiment, with the best performance achieving 81% top-1 accuracy. This was accomplished using an image size eight times larger than the original size. While this falls 10% short of the claim in the SimSiam paper, it's worth noting we achieved this result with a single GPU and without the use of mixed precision training tools.

The learning curve suggests that data size is pivotal not just in determining performance but also in influencing the speed of performance improvement or convergence. The initial 20 epochs reveal a noticeably improved rising trend and convergence speed. Moreover, although the overlay technique deviates from conventional augmentation methods in terms of data size, it doesn't induce a significant performance decrease or collapse as observed with previous adjustments to image size and CNN kernel size. Instead, the similarity loss remains stable as the accuracy incrementally rises throughout the training process.

We presented our findings from experiments conducted on supervised transfer learning and SSL with an overlay. In supervised transfer learning, we achieved high accuracy using ResNet-50 and ResNet-18 models on CIFAR-10, with a top accuracy of 97.55%. In SSL with SimSiam, we examined various setups, identifying combinations of image size and convolution kernel size that produced subpar results. However, the combination of the ResNet-18 encoder, original 32×32 image resolution, and a 3×3 convolution kernel, displayed satisfactory results. We also scrutinized the challenging nature of data augmentation and overlay in SSL, highlighting the role data augmentation plays in this context.

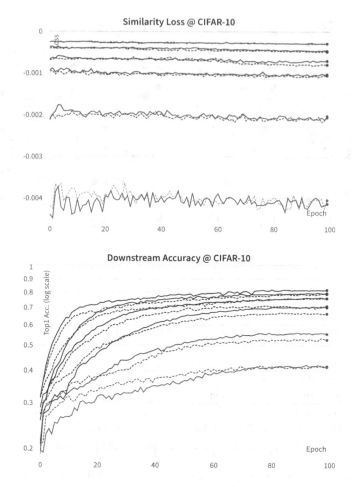

Fig. 5. Overlay and Extend with augmentation experiment results.

Lastly, we detailed the performance of overlay and extended-size augmentation data on ResNet-50 accuracy and presented the training processes and results from SimSiam experiments. The overlay technique has shown the potential to reduce the training dataset size without significantly compromising performance.

5 Conclusion

Our study has presented some intriguing observations regarding the role of augmentation dataset size in SSL performance and has revealed unexpected limitations regarding the overlay method's effectiveness in this context. We observed that augmenting the dataset size significantly boosts SSL performance, a finding that was not extensively explored in previous research. This discovery could potentially reshape the strategies employed in SSL by underlining the importance of using diverse and augmented data.

In contrast, the overlay method did not deliver the expected enhancements in the context of SSL tasks within our experiments. We should note that our investigations were constrained to direct image overlay without additional modifications, and it is plausible that the overlay technique could yield better results with refined implementation. This presents an interesting direction for future exploration, where the overlay method could be improved or combined with other techniques to fully leverage its potential in boosting SSL performance.

While our results with the overlay technique were not as promising as anticipated, we still believe this method holds the potential for further investigation. Future research endeavours could delve into refining the overlay technique, incorporating additional tweaks, or optimizing the method for more effective use in SSL.

To sum up, our research has shed light on the significance of dataset size in determining SSL performance and underscored the limitations of the overlay method as a standalone technique for data augmentation. These insights not only contribute to the broader understanding of SSL but could also guide future research efforts in devising novel methods to improve SSL performance. By persisting in the exploration and refinement of augmentation techniques, we can potentially unlock new avenues for advancements in SSL and its applications across various domains.

References

1. Asano, Y., Rupprecht, C., Vedaldi, A.: Self-labelling via simultaneous clustering and representation learning. In: International Conference on Learning Representations (2020)
2. Caron, M., Bojanowski, P., Mairal, J., Joulin, A.: Unsupervised pre-training of image features on non-curated data. In: Proceedings of the IEEE/CVF International Conference on Computer Vision, pp. 2959–2968 (2019)
3. Caron, M., Misra, I., Mairal, J., Goyal, P., Bojanowski, P., Joulin, A.: Unsupervised learning of visual features by contrasting cluster assignments. Adv. Neural. Inf. Process. Syst. **33**, 9912–9924 (2020)
4. Caron, M., Touvron, H., Misra, I., Jégou, H., Mairal, J., Bojanowski, P., Joulin, A.: Emerging properties in self-supervised vision transformers. In: Proceedings of the IEEE/CVF International Conference on Computer Vision, pp. 9650–9660 (2021)
5. Chen, T., Kornblith, S., Norouzi, M., Hinton, G.: A simple framework for contrastive learning of visual representations. In: International Conference on Machine Learning, pp. 1597–1607. PMLR (2020)
6. Chen, X., He, K.: Exploring simple siamese representation learning. In: Proceedings of the IEEE/CVF Conference on Computer Vision and Pattern Recognition, pp. 15750–15758 (2021)
7. Grill, J.B., et al.: Bootstrap your own latent-a new approach to self-supervised learning. Adv. Neural. Inf. Process. Syst. **33**, 21271–21284 (2020)
8. He, K., Fan, H., Wu, Y., Xie, S., Girshick, R.: Momentum contrast for unsupervised visual representation learning. In: Proceedings of the IEEE/CVF Conference on Computer Vision and Pattern Recognition, pp. 9729–9738 (2020)

9. He, K., Zhang, X., Ren, S., Sun, J.: Deep residual learning for image recognition. In: Proceedings of the IEEE Conference on Computer Vision and Pattern Recognition, pp. 770–778 (2016)

10. Hoffer, E., Ben-Nun, T., Hubara, I., Giladi, N., Hoefler, T., Soudry, D.: Augment your batch: improving generalization through instance repetition. In: Proceedings of the IEEE/CVF Conference on Computer Vision and Pattern Recognition, pp. 8129–8138 (2020)

11. Hua, T., Wang, W., Xue, Z., Ren, S., Wang, Y., Zhao, H.: On feature decorrelation in self-supervised learning. In: Proceedings of the IEEE/CVF International Conference on Computer Vision, pp. 9598–9608 (2021)

12. Huang, G., Sun, Yu., Liu, Z., Sedra, D., Weinberger, K.Q.: Deep networks with stochastic depth. In: Leibe, B., Matas, J., Sebe, N., Welling, M. (eds.) ECCV 2016. LNCS, vol. 9908, pp. 646–661. Springer, Cham (2016). https://doi.org/10.1007/978-3-319-46493-0_39

13. Jing, L., Vincent, P., LeCun, Y., Tian, Y.: Understanding dimensional collapse in contrastive self-supervised learning. In: International Conference on Learning Representations (2022)

14. Krizhevsky, A., Hinton, G., et al.: Learning multiple layers of features from tiny images. Technical report, Toronto, ON, Canada (2009)

15. Li, A.C., Efros, A.A., Pathak, D.: Understanding collapse in non-contrastive siamese representation learning. In: Computer Vision-ECCV 2022: 17th European Conference, Tel Aviv, Israel, October 23–27, 2022, Proceedings, Part XXXI, pp. 490–505. Springer (2022)

16. Purushwalkam, S., Gupta, A.: Demystifying contrastive self-supervised learning: invariances, augmentations and dataset biases. Adv. Neural. Inf. Process. Syst. **33**, 3407–3418 (2020)

17. Reed, C.J., Metzger, S., Srinivas, A., Darrell, T., Keutzer, K.: Selfaugment: automatic augmentation policies for self-supervised learning. In: Proceedings of the IEEE/CVF Conference on Computer Vision and Pattern Recognition, pp. 2674–2683 (2021)

18. Tang, L., Xiang, X., Zhang, H., Gong, M., Ma, J.: Divfusion: darkness-free infrared and visible image fusion. Inf. Fusion **91**, 477–493 (2023)

19. Yosinski, J., Clune, J., Bengio, Y., Lipson, H.: How transferable are features in deep neural networks? Advances in neural information processing systems 27 (2014)

20. Zhang, C., Zhang, K., Zhang, C., Pham, T.X., Yoo, C.D., Kweon, I.S.: How does simsiam avoid collapse without negative samples? a unified understanding with self-supervised contrastive learning. In: International Conference on Learning Representations (2022)

21. Zhou, T., Cheng, Q., Lu, H., Li, Q., Zhang, X., Qiu, S.: Deep learning methods for medical image fusion: a review. Computers in Biology and Medicine, p. 106959 (2023)

BoCB: Performance Benchmarking by Analysing Impacts of Cloud Platforms on Consortium Blockchain

Zhiqiang Huang[(⊠)], Saurabh Garg , Wenli Yang , Ankur Lohachab,
Muhammad Bilal Amin , and Byeong-Ho Kang

College of Sciences and Engineering, University of Tasmania, Hobart, Australia
zhiqiang.huang@utas.edu.au

Abstract. Consortium blockchain has recently witnessed unprecedented popularity due to its implicit features and potential capabilities. On the other hand, cloud computing has become a mature technology and has reshaped numerous other innovative technologies through its flexible and efficient on-demand computing services. Consortium blockchain's performance issues undermine its wider acceptance but unleashing the cloud's computing capabilities can help to develop the full potential of blockchain. In other words, cloud technology and blockchain's potential integration can be envisaged as a next-generation information technology, highly characterised by scalable and secure solutions, respectively. In this context, it is important to understand what benefits blockchain gains from cloud integration in terms of performance. This article presents a comprehensive, empirical analysis for an in-depth study of the performance of the blockchain, specifically consortium (but not limited to) implemented on the cloud, ranging from identifying potential performance bottlenecks, to configuring system parameters. Furthermore, this article presents a novel framework for blockchain on cloud benchmarking (BoCB) and implement it by a Hyperledger Fabric application on four different commercial Cloud platforms. The evaluation results of the blockchain performance on heterogeneous cloud platforms can help developers select the best possible configuration and resources to optimise their applications accordingly.

Keywords: Blockchain · Cloud Computing · Hyperledger Fabric · Performance Benchmark

1 Introduction

The recent decade has witnessed unprecedented development in blockchain technology across various domains ranging from cryptocurrency [1], to supply chain [2, 3]. The rapidly increasing number of blockchain-based platforms has paved the way for next-generation service, particularly in financial and distributed applications. Global Market Insights [4] predicts a 69% increase in the number of investments in blockchain between 2019 and 2025. However, blockchain's performance issues, especially its low throughput, poor scalability and high latency, undermine its broader acceptance in industrial

© The Author(s), under exclusive license to Springer Nature Singapore Pte Ltd. 2023
S. Wu et al. (Eds.): PKAW 2023, LNAI 14317, pp. 43–57, 2023.
https://doi.org/10.1007/978-981-99-7855-7_4

areas. Conventional technologies such as cloud computing can play a significant role in blockchain technology to improve its performance. Cloud computing indicates the fundamental element of the current digital world, which has already been developing at an extraordinary speed in the last decade.

Various industries argued that this decade could be the year of Blockchain as a Service (BaaS). It may seem obvious that a combination of Blockchain and Cloud technology will enable large-scale deployment and serve the ever-increasing demand for Blockchain. However, it is not clear whether such integration of Blockchain with Cloud will produce the required performance. In other words, a comprehensive benchmarking of Blockchain performance is needed for understanding suitable vendor and deployment configuration.

Previously, there have been several attempts to evaluate and benchmark Blockchain performance [5–14]. A variety of essential performance issues have been studied in the context of different Blockchains, such as Ethereum, Fabric, Sawtooth and so on, including the performance of the proof (be it work, stake or other), transaction processing and block creation. Recent blockchain performance benchmarking methods mainly focus on a private blockchain, with few considering consortium and public platforms. Although most of them are built on cloud platforms, they seldom consider effects of the cloud on their performance. Lack of blockchain performance benchmarking standards and tools, especially those involving cloud platform influencing factors, restricts its adoption. For example, in a cloud environment, computing capability like VM size can be scaled up and down to work as a flexible parameter before benchmarking. Benchmarking blockchain performance in a cloud environment is a comprehensive process because we must consider both the intrinsic properties of cloud and Blockchain, and their effects on each other.

In this context, we designed a novel blockchain performance benchmarking framework (BoCB: Blockchain on Cloud Benchmarking), which is comprised of four essential layers: blockchain platform layer, interface layer, adapter layer and performance evaluation layer. Utilising this framework, we investigate the blockchain's performance (that is, Hyperledger) services on multiple public cloud vendors such as IBM Azure and Google Cloud, using a mature benchmarking methodology called CEEM [15]. We establish a specific performance benchmarking methodology for cloud services and provided a systematic framework to perform evaluative studies that can be reproduced easily or extended for any cloud and blockchain environment. Our work chooses Hyperledger Fabric 1.43 as our blockchain experiment platforms for it is widely supported by almost all the major cloud providers, but the main novelty and contribution of our work is the benchmarking framework which firstly combine both blockchain and cloud sides parameters. This methodology can also easily be fulfilled in all the other consortium blockchain platforms, and even public or private blockchain environments.

In this paper, we designed a novel blockchain performance benchmarking framework (BoCB: Blockchain on Cloud Benchmarking) and deployed BoCB with its modelling on a heterogeneous cloud environment. We chose consortium blockchain as our research target and set up a clear overall workflow for our benchmarking steps. Then, a case study is illustrated by deploying Hyperledger Fabric on several cloud platforms (that is, IBM, Google, Amazon and Nectar) to investigate the feasibility of our proposed benchmarking framework.

2 Related Work

In general, we can consider performance benchmarking as a specially controlled performance evaluation because benchmarking tends to work in a standardised environment with a pre-documented workload. Only with benchmarks is the comparison between widely different backgrounds valuable. However, our research pays more attention to benchmark blockchain performance, based on its related metrics, rather than benchmarking. This is an essential step at the beginning, before any formal benchmark is developed and accepted by industries.

Performance studies for public Blockchains, in particular, have so far been restricted. For instance, the works [16, 17] provide a deep analysis of the impacts of block sizes and network broadcasting time on TPS. Some recently published papers attempt to improve the performance of Bitcoin [8, 13, 18] and focus only on the consensus layer, in which some benchmark tools, analysing models or network simulating systems, could be leveraged to assist these novel designs. Some types of overall performance evaluation methods [19–25] without detailed performance monitoring methods and they did not consider the interactions between different process stages. Similarly, some authors [26] structure blockchain into layers and applied the specific benchmarks to test them separately. However, the current version of Blockbench has no comparative evaluation for the core components of a blockchain and cannot support Fabric1.0 and any public blockchain at this time.

Some recent related works introduce some performance attributes for the blockchain system in both qualitative and quantitative ways and further modelled its metrics after investigation. For example, [27] posted a blockchain performance benchmarking framework, and designed and tested it in the Hyperledger Fabric 0.6 environment. In [28], authors designed a performance modelling framework that could simulate and predict blockchain behaviours to help blockchain evaluation and design. The objective of this framework is also to assist in the development of the blockchain in early stages. [29] also presented a blockchain performance benchmarking framework which was developed and built-in Hyperledger Fabric Version 0.6.

After investigating these related works, we find that many papers propose their characterised benchmarking or evaluating methods focusing on different blockchain features, with some similar performance metrics and benchmarking frameworks. A few of them consider the integration of the blockchain and the cloud and the impacts of cloud platforms, which really exist and could positively affect the blockchain's performance. To conclude, we extract the six most worthy papers for our research study and summarised them in Table 1. Considering the limitations of current related research work and papers, we focus more on studying the interactions between the blockchain system and the cloud platform, to determine the actual impacts of the cloud on blockchain performance and finally, we propose our novel benchmarking framework for blockchain on the cloud.

Table 1. Summary of the related works

Topics	Contributions	Performance Metrics	Limitations
Performance analysis of Hyperledger fabric platforms [30]	Hyperledger Fabric version 1.0 exceeds its previous version 0.6	throughput, latency, scalability and execution time	Use old Hyperledger Fabric with no cloud impacts consideration
Detailed and Real-time Performance Monitoring Framework for Blockchain [6]	Designed a log-based performance monitoring approach, with advantages of more details, real-time and reduced overhead	Overall: TPS, ARD, TPC, TPM, TPN; Detailed: RPC response rate, Contract execution time, state update time, consensus cost time	Log-based, without tracing system and anomaly detection
BLOCKBENCH: Framework for Analysing Private Blockchains [26]	First proposed evaluation framework to analyse private blockchains; can compare different blockchain platforms fairly and provide deep understanding of different blockchain design options	Macro benchmarks: Throughput, latency, scalability, fault tolerance; Micro benchmarks: execution layer, data model, consensus	Designed for private blockchain, Identify bottlenecks without solutions on the cloud
Performance Analysis of Consensus Algorithm in Private Blockchain [8]	Provided a model to evaluate consensus performance on private blockchains, Hyperledger Fabric and private Ethereum; with contributions: quantitative data supporting for future research of consensus algorithm; guiding blockchain users in selecting consensus algorithms	Latency and throughput	Focus on consensus algorithm performance without considering the impacts of other blockchain components and cloud platforms

(continued)

Table 1. (*continued*)

Topics	Contributions	Performance Metrics	Limitations
Performance Analysis of Private Blockchain Platforms in Varying Workloads [10]	Provided a performance analysis of two widely used private blockchain platforms: Ethereum and Hyperledger Fabric, to evaluate their performance and limitations under various workloads	Execution Time, Latency, Throughput	Designed for private blockchain, without considering public blockchain and code-level influence
Performance Benchmarking and Optimising Hyperledger Fabric Blockchain Platform [31]	Proposed a systematic and experimental analysis of the performance of a permissioned blockchain: Hyperledger Fabric. Identifying 3 main performance bottlenecks. Introducing six worthy guidelines to configure Fabric parameters for performance optimisation	Throughput Latency	Experiment on old Hyperledger Fabric platform without considering consensus and network impacts

3 Benchmarking Methodology

3.1 Experiment Framework and Performance Modelling

We develop and set up a clear overall workflow for our benchmarking steps, as shown in Fig. 1. It contains three parts, where the left part is on behalf of the cloud services' benchmarking workflow, the middle part is the benchmarking object, and the right part is the blockchain benchmarking methods.

Our testing blockchain applications are built on a cloud platform and provided as a service to customers. Considering this situation, we follow the CEEM [15], which is an established specific performance evaluation methodology for cloud services, including a systematic framework to perform benchmarking studies. Thus, we can quickly reproduce and extend CEEM in our experimental environment.

We select consortium blockchain as our benchmarking target in our current experimental stage, simply considering its widespread use and ease of implementation. To be precise, we select Hyperledger Fabric as our blockchain platform and analyse its performance by utilising a customised Hyperledger Caliper. Based on some common

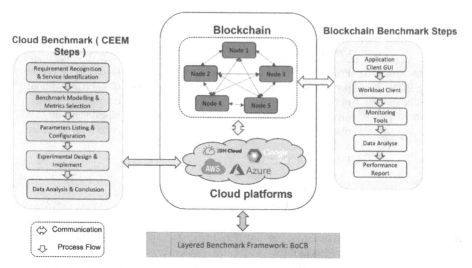

Fig. 1. Illustration of the workflow of the underlying Benchmarking framework

blockchain structures provided by different blockchain platforms and combine the CEEM steps, we designed our novel blockchain on cloud performance benchmarking framework (BoCB) as shown in Fig. 2. This performance of this blockchain platform's benchmark framework is comprised of four essential layers from bottom to top, as illustrated in Fig. 2, including the blockchain platform layer, interface layer, adapter layer and performance evaluation layer. Among them, the blockchain platform layer is built in the cloud environment. The adaptor layer is the most critical part of our framework, with the primary function of integrating various blockchain applications into this evaluation system. When these blockchain applications are evaluated, this adaptor layer takes the responsibility of communicating between the bottom blockchain protocol and the up-neighbour interface. The middle interface layer is designed for presenting various blockchain up-linked interfaces with the functions of deploying, invoking, and enquiring smart contracts. This layer is also responsible for monitoring system resources like CPU and memory. The top performance evaluation/benchmark layer is used to implement pressure tests on every deployed blockchain application.

Before blockchain performance benchmarking, we must model the performance metrics. We study the throughput and latency as the primary performance metrics for Fabric. Throughput is the rate at which transactions are committed to the ledger. Latency is the time taken from the application sending the transaction proposal to the transaction commit, and we select the average value as its primary index.

- **Average Throughput** is used to measure the number of successful transactions per second before testing configures a workload with multi-threads per client to fully load the blockchain throughput.

$$TPS_\mu = \frac{Count(Txsin(t_{i,}, t_j))}{t_j - t_i} \tag{1}$$

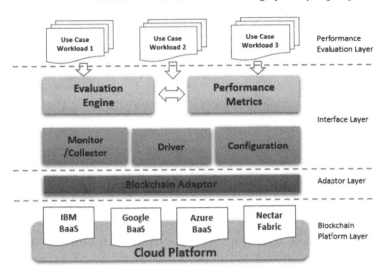

Fig. 2. Proposed Layered Benchmarking Framework: BoCB

- **Average Latency** is used to measure the response time per transaction before testing, using the driver to implement blocking transaction, and starting another just after finishing the previous one.

$$AVL_\mu = \frac{\sum_{Tx}(t_{TxComfirmed} - t_{TxInitated})}{Count(Txin(t_i, t_j))} \tag{2}$$

3.2 Applications and Scenarios Design

To implement our blockchain performance benchmarking in a cloud environment, we select appropriate representative cloud platforms to build our blockchain applications in the first step. After careful investigation, we finally choose four of the most popular commercial Cloud Service Providers (CSPs), which are three commercial CSPs (IBM, Microsoft Azure and Google) and one free research cloud (Nectar). Then we set up a blockchain application on the cloud platforms separately. Our experiment chose a digital assets management system as our blockchain benchmarking object. It is developed in Node.js and built on Fabric 1.4.4, with some essential digital assets' management functions. We utilise a customised blockchain monitoring tool to collect pre-defined performance key indices then report and analyse the experimental data. We took the IBM platform as an example, describing the detailed deployment steps in Fig. 3.

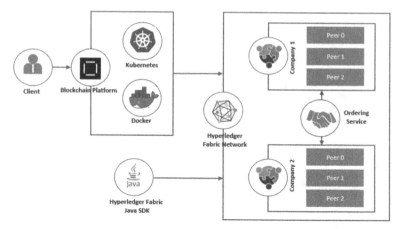

Fig. 3. A case study application scenario implemented on Hyperledger Fabric

3.3 Configuration and Workload

Our benchmark configuration is comprised of three main parts: workload setting, system setting and cloud setting.

Workload Setting: Workload modules are the essence of our benchmark since it is their responsibility to construct and submit TXs. To implement the workload module, we customise the Node.JS API provided by the open-source Caliper. Our workload module exports the following three asynchronous functions: init(), run() and end().

The *'init'* function is called before a round is started. It receives the SUT adapter instance in the blockchain parameter, the adapter-specific context created by the adapter, usually containing additional data about the network. The *'run'* function is called every time the set rate controller enables the next TX. The *'end'* function is called after the round has ended. To perform a benchmark test, we run several worker processes to generate the workload and run one master process to coordinate the different testing rounds among these worker processes. This process involves four parameters to be configured in advance: Clients number $F(X_1)$, TXs number $F(X_2)$, Send Rate $F(X_3)$ and Rounds $F(X_4)$. These four are combined to define the experiment workload.

- **Clients' Number** refers to the number of client sub-processes launched by each peer node. The total client number could be counted as F(X1) *Peer Nodes Number.
- **MaxMessageCount:** We configure it as one of the crucial factors of the block size. The other two factors are predefined in fabric configuration by BatchTimeOut and MaxMessageCount. We set it as a flexible parameter and change it linearly to watch the performance changes with block size.
- **Sending Rate:** Considering our available experimental environment and budget limitations, we set up the TXs sending rate, ranging from $20 \sim 6000$, depending on different system configurations.
- **Rounds:** Considering the performance of different blockchain functions, we set up at least two rounds to perform our experiment: Operation Round and Query Round.

Operation Round involves opening an account and initialising it or updating its value. The Query Round just does the simple query in the blockchain application for an existing account. For each round, Total TXs number sent by clients can be calculated by the formula: Peer Node Number * F(X1) *F(X3).

System Setting: involves Fabric related configuration corresponding to the blockchain application's internal business and functional requirements. We utilise three organisations and two peers for each, with their CAs and Orderers for our digital assets management system. Three organisations with two peers could simulate and represent most of the typical blockchain applications and be easily performed and maintained. We select the most stable and suitable version to perform our tests for each experimental environment component. Mostly, the best one is not the latest one (Table 2).

Table 2. Overall considered system under test.

Items	Version	Reason for Use
Hyperledger Fabric	1.4.3	Stable release [32]
Operation System	Ubuntu Linux 20.04 LTS Focal	Latest and stable
Benchmark Tools	Caliper 0.2.0	Stable release
Node.js	8.13.0	Suitable for Caliper 0.2.0 [28]
NPM	6.4.1	Suitable for Caliper 0.2.0
GO	1.14.2	Latest and stable
Docker	19.03.13	Latest and stable

To simulate the complicated real world well and to consider the convenience of the experimental operation, we set up our Fabric system as shown in the following Table 3.

Table 3. An example configuration of the one node in experimentation

Items	Version	Reason for Use
Hyperledger Fabric	1.4.3	Stable release
Organisation Number	2, 3	Suitable for most business requirement
Peers Number	6	Distribution testing required
CA Number	1, 2	Distribution testing required
Channel	1	Satisfy the requirements and easy to maintain
Orderer Number	1	Satisfy the requirements and easy to maintain
Consensus	Kafka	Fabric latest consensus
BatchTime Out	1 s–3 s	Flexible for block size
MaxMessageCount	1000–6000	Flexible for block size

Cloud Platform Setting: This part of the setting involves VMs, Dockers, Kubernetes, Storages and Networks resources allocation in the cloud platforms. To achieve the best performance of blockchain on a cloud, we test its changes based on different cloud configurations.

Table 4. Cloud Platform Setting

Platforms	VM Size
• Nectar	• VM1: 1vCPUs 4G Mem 30G Disk;
• IBM	• VM2: 2vCPUs 8G Mem 30G Disk;
• Microsoft Azure	• VM3: 4vCPUs 16G Mem 30G Disk;
• Google	• VM4: 8vCPUs 32G Mem 30G Disk

Config and Workload Steps: In our work, we are more concerned with the trend of performance over these parameters and its change in a medium scale. A brief configuration and workload process are:

• Launch the VM instances on cloud, which could be resized later. Setup the private virtual network and authorise the required access right.
• Deploy the customised blockchain and caliper application on the VMs.
• Config orderers, CAs, organisations, peers, and their hosts and IP addresses.
• Config client number, TXs number, TPS and Rounds.
• Initiate a benchmark run by utilising five worker processes.
• Predefine two rounds to perform the test: operation and query. The first operation round submits 1000 TXs at a 300 TPS send rate. The second query round submits 1000 TXs at a fixed 300 TPS send rate.
• The content of the TXs is determined by the operation.js and query.js workload module.
• The master process observes the progress of the worker every five seconds and generates the performance reports.

4   Results and Analysis

Our case study designed several representative scenarios and deployed them distinctively on selected different cloud platforms to identify the difference in blockchain performance in various cloud environments. We conduct two kinds of comparisons: horizontal and vertical comparisons.

• **Horizontal comparison** is used to compare the blockchain performance on different cloud platforms, such as IBM, Azure, Google and Nectar, based on the same application scenarios. This comparison's direct and straightforward use presents one critical factor of BaaS ranking and helps customers to select appropriate cloud platforms.

- **Vertical comparison** can be considered as a kind of cloud-wise internal comparison, which compares the blockchain performances based on different resource allocations within the same cloud platform. This type of comparison helps the blockchain developers select or scale the cloud resources to pursue the application's best performance. It is an essential basis for and means of blockchain performance optimisation on a cloud.

4.1 Horizontal Comparison

Case 1: Comparison Based on VM Size

Firstly, we scale up the virtual machine's computing size, including vCPU number, memory and disk sizes, to implement the same blockchain application in the cloud environment. Four levels of the sizes are selected and named from VM1 to VM4 shown in Table 4.

As per the experimental data in this section, we can find that all the blockchain performances on these four cloud platforms present a similar trend, referring to improving when VM size is scaled up. However, the degrees are slightly different. In this case, in terms of average latency performance, Google is a little better than Azure, then IBM and the last one is Nectar. For throughput performance, IBM is the best, then Google is very similar to Azure, and the last one is Nectar, as shown in Fig. 4. It is easy to understand that commercial cloud platforms typically provide better services than free ones for utilising optimised hardware and software cloud infrastructures. In conclusion, scaling the VM size is an efficient way to improve blockchain performance on the cloud platform.

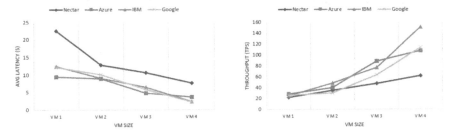

Fig. 4. Performance results (i.e., Avg. Latency, and Throughput) based on VM Size

Case 2: Comparison Based on Block Size

Block size is an essential factor that influences blockchain performance. We select MaxMessageCount as our block size configuration parameters and set five rounds to test, with the values 5, 10, 20, 50, 100 separately.

Generally, blockchain on the IBM cloud platform performs better than that on Microsoft Azure, followed by Google and Nectar platforms. In addition, they all change in the same trend, which means performance improves when blocking size increases. In this situation, when the MaxMessageCount exceeds 50, the improvement slows. After the value surpasses 100, the TPS can only increase a little and finally reaches its maximum of 238 by IBM cloud with 8vCPU and 32GMem in the operation round. To sum up, IBM performs better than Azure, then Google and Nectar (Fig. 5).

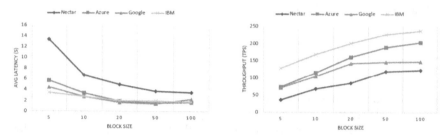

Fig. 5. Performance results (i.e., Avg. Latency, and Throughput) based on block size.

4.2   Vertical Comparison

Case 1: Based on vCPU Number and Memory Size

In this case, we perform 4 benchmarking tests on each cloud platform by scaling up the vCPU number and Memory size in four predefined levels: one vCPUs 4G Mem (VM1), two vCPUs 8G Mem (VM2), four vCPUs 8G Mem (VM3) and eight vCPUs 32G Mem (VM4). We test two main business functions, such as transfer and query, by predefined workloads. After three rounds of tests, we collect primary TPS and Latency data and illustrate them in the following figure (using Netcar as example in Fig. 6).

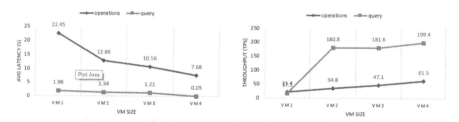

Fig. 6. Performance of the blockchain on Netcar cloud platforms based on the VM size.

Analysing the graphs and data from each cloud platform, we find a common trend among all the cloud platforms. The average latency for the operating function decreased dramatically when we scaled up the VM computing sizes, significantly when it increased from two CPUs 4GMem to four vCPUs 8GMem. In contrast, the throughputs did increase but rarely. For the query function part, its average latency decreased, and throughput increased too. We could conclude that scaling up the VM size in the cloud platform can significantly improve blockchain performance. Additionally, the slope of the curves could reveal the scalability of the blockchain on the cloud while the VM size changes.

Case 2: Based on Block Size
As per the results in Fig. 7, we find that the performance is improved when increasing the block sizes in all the scenarios on four cloud platforms. There are several ways for Fabric application to modify the block size: BatchTimeout, /dsex, AbsoluteMaxBytes and PreferredMaxBytes. Considering our blockchain application is a simple one without big-size transactions and operation convenience, we select MaxMessageCount as our block size configuration parameters. Taking the Nectar cloud platform as an example, the above figures illustrate that the average latency of the operation round decreases from 17.72 to 3.44, and its throughput increases from 6.6 tps to 122 tps.

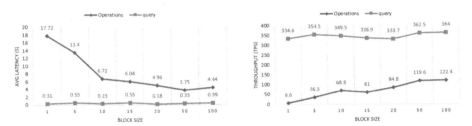

Fig. 7. Performance of the blockchain on Nectar cloud based on the block size.

5 Conclusion and Future Work

According to the experimental results in this stimulated environment, we find that the cloud-based consortium blockchain application can easily and systematically be benchmarked with our proposed BoCB benchmarking framework and effectively optimised by adjusting system parameters and reallocating the resources appropriately, such as scaling up the VM size and distributing the blockchain functions on more hosts. The BoCB benchmarking framework can be utilised well in this combination environment and can assist developers to improve their blockchain performance on the cloud. There is no doubt that the rapidly growing BaaS market and the trend of integrating blockchain with the cloud stimulate the research focus on precise blockchain performance benchmarking which primarily conducted in a cloud environment.

Our current work presented a feasible benchmarking framework (BoCB) for cloud-based consortium blockchain performance and justified it in Hyperledger Fabric platforms. BoCB can help blockchain developers to select and assess properly cloud services utilised in their blockchain systems to achieve high application performance. On the other hand, it also provides a specific benchmarking tool for cloud providers to monitor their services and finally, it offers high-quality blockchain services to customers. After this, our further work is to optimise blockchain performance by adequately using the cloud's ubiquitous resources. We plan to concentrate on 1) extending the benchmarking method from consortium blockchain to public blockchain; 2) utilising the enforced benchmarking tool to monitor blockchain performance across the whole cloud and identifying the bottlenecks in blockchain performance, and 3) designing a cloud resource reallocating algorithm to eliminate the bottleneck and rescale cloud services automatically in terms of the best blockchain performance.

References

1. Lee, J.Y.: A decentralized token economy: How blockchain and cryptocurrency can revolutionize business. Bus. Horiz.Horiz. **62**(6), 773–784 (2019)
2. Korpela, K., Hallikas, J., Dahlberg, T.: Digital supply chain transformation toward blockchain integration. In: Proceedings of the 50th Hawaii International Conference on System Sciences (2017)
3. Yafimava, D.: Blockchain In the Supply Chain: 10 Real-Life Use Cases and Examples (2019). https://openledger.info/insights/blockchain-in-the-supply-chain-use-cases-examples/
4. Ankita Bhutani, P.W.: Blockchain Technology Market Size By Providers. 2019: Global Market Insights
5. Smetanin, S., et al.: Blockchain evaluation approaches: state-of-the-art and future perspective. Sensors **20**(12) (2020)
6. Zheng, P., et al.: A detailed and real-time performance monitoring framework for blockchain systems. In: 2018 IEEE/ACM 40th International Conference on Software Engineering: Software Engineering in Practice Track (ICSE-SEIP) (2018)
7. Suankaewmanee, K., et al.: Performance analysis and application of mobile blockchain. In: 2018 International Conference on Computing, Networking and Communications (ICNC). IEEE (2018)
8. Hao, Y., et al.: Performance analysis of consensus algorithm in private blockchain. In: 2018 IEEE Intelligent Vehicles Symposium (IV). IEEE (2018)
9. Nasir, Q., et al.: Performance analysis of hyperledger fabric platforms. Secur. Commun. Networks **2018**, 3976093 (2018)
10. Pongnumkul, S., Siripanpornchana, C., Thajchayapong, S.: Performance analysis of private blockchain platforms in varying workloads. In: 2017 26th International Conference on Computer Communication and Networks (ICCCN). IEEE (2017)
11. Quanxin, Z.: Performance Analysis of the Blockchain Based on Markovian Chain. China Academic Journal Electonic Publishing House (2019)
12. Fan, C., et al.: Performance evaluation of blockchain systems: a systematic survey. IEEE Access, 1 (2020)
13. Sukhwani, H., et al.: Performance modeling of PBFT consensus process for permissioned blockchain network (Hyperledger Fabric). In: 2017 IEEE 36th Symposium on Reliable Distributed Systems (SRDS) (2017)
14. Bamakan, S.M.H., Motavali, A., Babaei Bondarti, A.: A survey of blockchain consensus algorithms performance evaluation criteria. Expert Syst. Appl., **154**, p. 113385 (2020)
15. Li, Z., OBrien, L., Zhang, H.: CEEM: a practical methodology for cloud services evaluation. In: 2013 IEEE Ninth World Congress on Services. IEEE (2013)
16. Decker, C., Wattenhofer, R.: Information propagation in the bitcoin network. In: IEEE P2P 2013 Proceedings. IEEE (2013)
17. Croman, K., et al.: On scaling decentralized blockchains. in International conference on financial cryptography and data security. Springer (2016)
18. Gervais, A., et al.: On the security and performance of proof of work blockchains. In: Proceedings of the 2016 ACM SIGSAC Conference on Computer and Communications Security. ACM (2016)

19. Weber, I., et al.: On availability for blockchain-based systems. In: 2017 IEEE 36th Symposium on Reliable Distributed Systems (SRDS). IEEE (2017)
20. Kalodner, H., et al.: BlockSci: design and applications of a blockchain analysis platform. arXiv preprint arXiv:1709.02489 (2017)
21. Luu, L., et al.: Making smart contracts smarter. In: Proceedings of the 2016 ACM SIGSAC Conference on Computer and Communications Security (2016)
22. Chen, W., et al.: Detecting ponzi schemes on ethereum: towards healthier blockchain technology. In: Proceedings of the 2018 World Wide Web Conference. 2018
23. Bhargavan, K., et al.: Formal verification of smart contracts: Short paper. In: Proceedings of the 2016 ACM Workshop on Programming Languages and Analysis for Security (2016)
24. Marino, B., Juels, A.: Setting standards for altering and undoing smart contracts. in International Symposium on Rules and Rule Markup Languages for the Semantic Web. Springer (2016)
25. Chen, T., et al.: Under-optimized smart contracts devour your Money. In: 2017 IEEE 24th International Conference on Software Analysis, Evolution and Reengineering (SANER). IEEE (2017)
26. Dinh, T.T.A., et al.: Blockbench: a framework for analyzing private blockchains. In: Proceedings of the 2017 ACM International Conference on Management of Data (2017). ACM
27. Koteska, B., Karafiloski, E., Mishev, A.: Blockchain implementation quality challenges: a literature. In: SQAMIA 2017: 6th Workshop of Software Quality, Analysis, Monitoring, Improvement, and Applications (2017)
28. Yasaweerasinghelage, R., Staples, M., Weber, I.: Predicting latency of blockchain-based systems using architectural modelling and simulation. In: 2017 IEEE International Conference on Software Architecture (ICSA). IEEE (2017)
29. Kocsis, I., et al.: Towards performance modeling of hyperledger fabric. In: International IBM Cloud Academy Conference (ICACON) (2017)
30. Nasir, Q., et al.: Performance analysis of hyperledger fabric platforms. Security and Communication Networks (2018). **2018**
31. Thakkar, P., Nathan, S., Viswanathan, B.: Performance benchmarking and optimizing hyperledger fabric blockchain platform. In: 2018 IEEE 26th International Symposium on Modeling, Analysis, and Simulation of Computer and Telecommunication Systems (MASCOTS). IEEE (2018)
32. Calero, J.M.A., et al.: Comparative analysis of architectures for monitoring cloud computing infrastructures. Future Gener. Comput. Syst. **47**(C), 16–30 (2015)

Automated Cattle Behavior Classification Using Wearable Sensors and Machine Learning Approach

Niken Prasasti Martono[1(✉)], Rie Sawado[2], Itoko Nonaka[2], Fuminori Terada[2], and Hayato Ohwada[1]

[1] Department of Industrial Systems Engineering, Tokyo University of Science, Noda, Japan
{niken,ohwada}@rs.tus.ac.jp
[2] Institute of Livestock and Grassland Science, National Agriculture and Food Research Organization, Tsukuba, Japan
{sawado,witoko69}@affrc.go.jp, teradafuminori@gmail.com

Abstract. This paper focuses on automating the classification of in-house cattle behavior using collar tags equipped with tri-axial accelerometers to collect data on feeding and ruminating behaviors. The accelerometer data is divided into time intervals (10, 30, 60, and 180 s), and we extract 15 essential posture-related features to create a labeled dataset for behavior classification. We evaluate four machine learning algorithms (Random Forest, Extreme Gradient Boosting, Decision Tree, and Logistic Regression) on this dataset using leave-one-out cross-validation. The results indicate that shorter time intervals result in better prediction performance. Random Forest and Decision Tree algorithms perform well, striking a good balance between sensitivity and specificity. This proposed approach holds promise for real-time behavior classification and has the potential to benefit livestock management and enhance animal welfare.

Keywords: Sensor data · Machine learning · Animal behavior classification · Precision agriculture

1 Introduction

By observing and analyzing cattle behavior, valuable insights can be obtained to improve livestock management and enhance animal welfare. This data not only enables the evaluation of animal health and welfare but also supports real-time resource management optimization. Relying solely on human labor for data collection can be costly and impractical, particularly when monitoring a large number of animals across extensive areas continuously. To tackle this challenge, wearable and networked sensor technologies play a pivotal role, offering an automated approach for efficiently gathering and processing relevant data.

Advancements in sensor technologies have brought about a revolution in the field of livestock management. Researchers have explored the use of wearable sensors, such as accelerometers [4,17], GPS trackers [5,14,15], and RFID

S. Wu et al. (Eds.): PKAW 2023, LNAI 14317, pp. 58–69, 2023.
https://doi.org/10.1007/978-981-99-7855-7_5

tags [16], to automatically monitor and collect data on cattle behavior. These sensors can provide information on movement patterns, activity levels, feeding behavior, and more. By attaching sensors to cattle, data can be collected continuously and remotely, reducing the need for constant human observation. Numerous studies have delved into specific aspects of cattle behavior, including grazing patterns, social interactions, and stress indicators. Some research has investigated the correlation between behavior and environmental factors, such as temperature [12], humidity [11], and pasture quality. Others have examined the impact of behavioral changes on the overall health and productivity of the herd [10].

This paper introduces a novel approach to analyzing cattle behavior, with a specific focus on cattle housed indoors. The study primarily emphasizes two critical behavior categories: feeding and ruminating. These behaviors hold significant importance in livestock management, as they directly influence animal health, productivity, and welfare, as noted by Antanaitis (2023) [1]. Examining feeding behavior provides insights into the nutritional intake and overall health of cattle, as highlighted in the work by King et al. (2018) [10]. It helps ensure that the animals receive an adequate and balanced diet, essential for optimal growth and production. Conversely, ruminating behavior serves as a vital indicator of animals' digestive health and overall well-being. Ruminating is a natural process in cattle where they regurgitate and re-chew their food to aid in proper digestion, as explained by Paudyal et al. (2021) [13]. Monitoring ruminating behavior helps identify potential digestive issues or discomfort in the animals.

What sets this study apart is its innovative methodology for classifying in-house cattle behavior. This method involves the use of wearable sensors and networked technologies integrated into collar tags attached to the cattle, enabling the capture of tri-axial accelerometer data. This approach not only provides valuable insights into head poses, which serve as indicators of ruminating behavior but also quantifies the intensity of body movement, which is indicative of feeding activities. Additionally, the approach involves calculating posture-related features, derived from the mean values of accelerometer outputs along three axes. Similarly, intensity features are determined through the average of the absolute values of each axis's outputs. This efficient computational strategy is essential for real-time behavioral analysis within resource-constrained environments.

1.1   Animals and Data Collection

Between October 2022 and December 2022, a trial was conducted at The Institute of Livestock and Grassland Science, National Agricultural Research Organization in Ibaraki Prefecture, Japan. This trial involved nine randomly selected cattle, each equipped with collar tags, as shown in Fig. 1(a), referred to as "its Bell," to collect a diverse set of data. These collar tags contained an MC3630 3-axis accelerometer sensor, which measured acceleration in three perpendicular spatial directions. Attached to the top of the animals' necks and secured with a collar belt, as illustrated in Fig. 1(b), the tags' X-axis measured forward/backward motion, the Y-axis denoted horizontal/sideways movement, and the Z-axis indicated upward/downward motion. The tri-axial accelerometer captured 12-bit integers at a sampling rate of 14 samples per second.

Cattle activity on a typical day follows their regular schedule and feeding times. In the morning, from 0840 h to 0940 h, cows engage in milking, an essential routine to extract milk for production purposes. In the evening, between 1600 and 1800 h, the cows are again led to a holding area, where they await their second milking session. Apart from milking, while outside, the cows are assumed to engage in typical bovine behaviors such as grazing, resting, and socializing within the herd. In addition to their regular activities, cows have specific feeding times throughout the day. They are fed at 0900 and 1800 h, with two more feeding sessions occurring during the night at 2230 and 0330 h, ensuring a constant supply of nutrients to support their health and milk production.

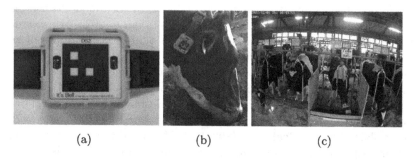

(a)   (b)   (c)

Fig. 1. Components of system installed in the barn: (a) accelerometer device; (b) accelerometer in the cattle's collar; (c) barn's camera view.

To facilitate night-time recording, a surveillance camera equipped with infrared vision was installed around the barn. The tagged cattle underwent continuous monitoring during the data collection phase, with their behavior recorded 24 h a day. The recording duration varied across different days for each cow. To document these observations, a video camera was strategically positioned near the animals. Subsequently, the recorded footage was used to annotate the corresponding accelerometer data obtained from the tags. The primary focus of the research was to annotate three distinct behaviors in cows: feeding (whether the cow was standing or lying down), ruminating (whether the cow was standing or lying down), and other behaviors. The "other" behaviors category encompassed a range of activities, including walking, resting, sleeping, drinking, grooming, and urinating. It is important to note that the recording of ruminating behavior was limited to instances where it persisted for more than 60 s and was specifically defined as "a cow standing or lying down, regurgitating, and chewing a bolus in a rhythmic manner" [6].

Identifying rare behaviors posed a particular challenge, even for experienced observers, due to their infrequent occurrence and swift nature. Furthermore, there were instances of ambiguity, such as short periods of rest or drinking during ruminating, or vice versa, which were not easily distinguishable from the recorded video. Additionally, during periods of rest or, to some extent, ruminating, whether standing or lying down, the cattle exhibited subtle movements of their heads, ear flicks, or muscle twitches. These occurrences were carefully observed and labeled as "other" behavior. Table 1 provides an illustration of the durations and behaviors derived from video footage observations of one animal over a week. It is important to note that the total time of annotated activities does not equate to the full 24 h or 86,400 s per day due to the presence of other activities beyond the recorded barn footage. Furthermore, the recorded video duration varies for each animal. However, all available and relevant video segments with clear distinctions between different activities are utilized in the analysis.

Table 1. Duration and behaviors of a cattle sample obtained by observing video footage over a one-week period (in seconds).

Day	Feeding	Ruminating	Other
1	21,744	19,577	23,365
2	23,738	21,703	26,040
3	25,137	22,691	24,687
4	23,659	18,866	26,849
5	21,502	23,502	22,324
6	23,983	25,814	24,349
7	20,675	16,299	10,605

1.2 Dataset

Data were collected using the provided sensor software, and the output was generated in the form of a Comma-Separated Values (CSV) file. Each row in the file corresponded to a unique timestamp, recorded in the format of date, hour, minute, second, and hundredths of a second. This row contained acceleration values for the X, Y, and Z axes, with each axis reported in separate columns. Subsequently, the CSV file was imported into Microsoft Excel for further analysis. Notably, any observed changes in cattle posture or behavior were manually annotated next to the corresponding acceleration values for each time interval.

In this study, our goal is to create a labeled dataset for classifying cattle behavior using accelerometer data. Each accelerometer reading, denoted as a_i, is initially associated with a corresponding behavioral label L_i, such as "feeding" or "ruminating." To process these readings, we employ non-overlapping sliding windows with varying durations: 10, 30, 60, and 180 s. These durations were chosen based on both existing literature and our empirical testing. The raw accelerometer readings over the time period can be represented as a set $A = \{a_1, a_2, \ldots, a_N\}$, where N is the total number of readings, and t_i is the time at which each reading a_i is taken.

For each window size W, we segment A into sets $S_W = \{s_1, s_2, \ldots, s_M\}$. Here, M is determined by $M = \lfloor \frac{N}{W} \rfloor$. Each set s_j comprises W consecutive readings, denoted as $s_j = \{a_{(j-1) \times W + 1}, a_{(j-1) \times W + 2}, \ldots, a_{j \times W}\}$. Following this segmentation, we extract various features from each s_j using a feature extraction function $F(s_j)$, which includes statistical measures such as the mean and standard deviation of the readings within the window. Consequently, the final labeled dataset D consists of pairs of feature vectors and their corresponding labels: $D = \{(F(s_1), L_1), (F(s_2), L_2), \ldots, (F(s_M), L_M)\}$.

To derive valuable insights from the annotated accelerometer data, we created plots that represent recorded activity for each behavior class and axis. In Fig. 2, we provide an illustration of sample accelerometer data comparing recorded feeding activity to other activities. Notably, for in-house cattle where the feeder position remains constant (Fig. 1(c)), feeding events are characterized by significantly higher movement intensity and variations in accelerometer readings. Conversely, when ruminating occurs, the accelerometer data reveals a more stable pattern of movement, with a noticeable increase in movement along the Z-axis, while the Y-axis typically records minimal movement, as shown in Fig. 3.

In this analysis, we extract a diverse set of 15 essential features from the accelerometer data to gain profound insights into the recorded movement patterns. These features are adapted from previous works [2,3,6], where they have been employed in analyzing cows and their behavior in free-range environments. However, in this paper, we apply these features to an in-house cattle management scenario. Each feature plays an indispensable role in deciphering the complexities of accelerometer data, providing a comprehensive framework for quantifying and interpreting various cattle behaviors. For instance, the mean values along the X, Y, and Z axes serve as critical indicators of central tendencies, offering a baseline for typical activities in different movement directions. This baseline becomes especially valuable when contrasted with the minimum and maximum values for each axis, revealing the lower and upper bounds of movement variability and highlighting any outliers or deviations that may indicate atypical behavior. The range along each axis further elaborates on this variability, offering insights into the range of movements and potential fluctuations in behavior.

In addition, features like the mean intensity offer an aggregate measure of the animal's overall activity levels, enabling us to assess the intensity and variation of movement patterns. These measurements are pivotal for distinguishing between different types of activities, each with its unique signature in the accelerometer data. The mean variation also plays a significant role, capturing the average rate of change in the cow's movements along each axis and serving as an early alert system for erratic or unusual behavior. Finally, the mean entropy contributes a nuanced layer to our understanding by quantifying the complexity and randomness of the recorded movements. This is invaluable for discerning the intricacies and subtleties of cattle behavior, from grazing to walking to more complex activities. By combining these features and correlating them with their timestamps, we assemble both training and test datasets that allow us to effectively analyze and classify cattle behavior in in-house settings using wearable sensors and accelerometer data. The formula and description of each feature are shown in Table 2.

Table 2. Description of features.

Feature	Description
Average of X , Y, Z axis	$mean_x = \frac{1}{n}\sum_{t=1}^{n} x(t), mean_y = \frac{1}{n}\sum_{t=1}^{n} y(t), mean_z = \frac{1}{n}\sum_{t=1}^{n} z(t)$
Minimum X, Y, Z axis	min_x, min_y, min_z
Maximum X, Y, Z axis	max_x, max_y, max_z
Range X, Y, Z axis	$range_x = max_x - min_x, range_y = max_y - min_y, range_z = max_z - min_z$
Mean intensity	$movintensity_{avg} = \frac{1}{n}\sum_{i=1}^{n} \sqrt{x_i^2 + y_i^2 + z_i^2}$
Mean variation	$movvariation_{avg} = \frac{1}{n}\sum_{i=1}^{n} \sqrt{(\Delta x_i)^2 + (\Delta y_i)^2 + (\Delta z_i)^2}$
Mean entropy	$moventropy_{avg} = \frac{1}{n}\sum_{t=1}^{n} ((1+x(t)+y(t)+z(t)^2)) \times ln(1 + x(t) + y(t) + z(t))$

1.3   Machine Learning Algorithm and Evaluation

In the evaluation of four machine learning algorithms, namely Random Forest (RF) [9], Extreme Gradient Boosting (XGB) [7], Decision Tree (DT) [18], and Logistic Regression (LR) [8], we considered the characteristics and strengths of each method. RF is an ensemble learning approach that combines DTs to enhance predictive accuracy and handle high-dimensional datasets. XGB, another ensemble method, iteratively builds trees to correct errors and prioritizes informative features for improved performance. DTs, while interpretable, can be prone to overfitting compared to ensemble methods. LR, a widely used classification algorithm, models the probability of binary outcomes but might struggle with capturing complex feature interactions.

The decision to use these four machine learning algorithms was based on several factors: (1) Computational efficiency: Algorithms like RF and Gradient Boosting are generally computationally efficient and can handle large datasets well. Time-series methods can sometimes be computationally intensive, which might not be ideal for real-time analysis, particularly in settings with limited computational resources; (2) Ease of interpretability: Methods like DTs and LR provide easier interpretability. In domains like livestock behavior analysis, being able to easily interpret and explain your model's decisions can be very valuable, especially for stakeholders who may not be machine learning experts; and (3) Model robustness: Non-time series algorithms like RF and Gradient Boosting can be less sensitive to noise and more robust to overfitting, especially when dealing with complex and noisy data, which is often the case in real-world settings like in-house cattle monitoring. Additionally, the nature of the data does not exhibit strong temporal dependencies that would warrant the use of time-series algorithms. For example, the behaviors being classified are relatively distinct and do not require an understanding of long-term temporal dynamics; traditional machine learning algorithms suffice.

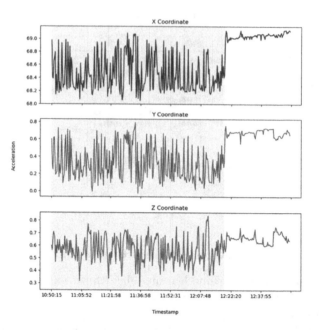

Fig. 2. Accelerometer data showing "feeding" activity (highlighted in yellow) vs. "other" activity. (Color figure online)

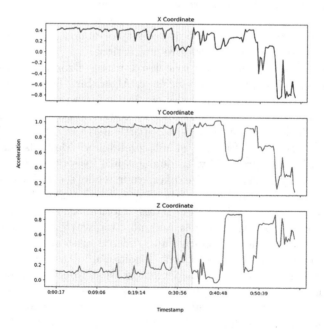

Fig. 3. Accelerometer data showing "ruminating" activity (highlighted in yellow) vs. "other" activity. (Color figure online)

Understanding their specific advantages and limitations is crucial for selecting the most suitable algorithm based on the dataset and problem requirements. For each machine learning method and time window, we calculated the average accuracy, sensitivity (recall), specificity, and precision using the following formulas:

$$\text{Accuracy} = \frac{TP + TN}{TP + TN + FP + FN}$$

$$\text{Precision} = \frac{TP}{TP + FP}$$

$$\text{Sensitivity (recall)} = \frac{TP}{TP + FN}$$

$$\text{Specificity} = \frac{TN}{TN + FP}$$

The leave-one-out cross-validation method was utilized to construct the training and testing sets for the model. This involved dividing the data from nine animals into nine iterations, with one animal's data excluded for testing, and the data from the remaining eight animals used for training in each iteration. This process was repeated nine times, with a different animal's data excluded each time for testing. By employing this approach, we thoroughly assessed the model's performance across all individual animals in the experiment.

2 Classification Results

In this section, we assess the performance of various machine learning models in forecasting animal behavior. The data presented in Table 3 indicate that the effectiveness of these models is closely related to the length of the time window used for analysis. Specifically, the models tend to perform better when shorter time intervals-10 s and 30 s-are considered. This suggests that short-term data segments contain more actionable information for accurate behavior categorization. Notably, the DT model stands out for its excellent performance in the 30-second time window, achieving the highest scores in both accuracy (**0.821**) and sensitivity (**0.870**). This result suggests that DT is highly proficient in recognizing behavioral patterns within this specific time frame. Therefore, for use cases that require high accuracy and sensitivity, it is advisable to employ a DT model based on 30-second intervals.

The RF algorithm consistently exhibits robust performance across various metrics, especially excelling in specificity, where it attains an impressive score of **0.915** at the 10-second interval. This outstanding performance can be attributed to RF's ensemble nature. It leverages multiple DTs, aggregating their predictions, which effectively mitigates the risk of overfitting and reduces variance. This ensemble architecture results in a more robust model capable of capturing the nuances and complexities in the data. Furthermore, RF's inherent ability to perform feature selection likely played a crucial role in achieving high specificity. By assigning higher importance to features that genuinely contribute to class separation, the algorithm effectively reduces the chances of misclassification, thereby lowering the rate of false positives. This attribute is especially valuable in applications that demand high precision, such as automated systems in livestock management. In such scenarios, a false positive could lead to resource wastage or incorrect behavioral interventions. Therefore, the strong performance of RF, particularly in specificity, makes it a valuable choice for these applications.

Lastly, the performance of XGB and LR varies depending on the time window. XGB exhibits promising results at the 30-second window, but its performance lags at the 180-second interval. This suggests that XGB may not be the ideal choice for longer-term behavior prediction. Similarly, LR competes well at shorter time intervals but experiences a performance drop when the window is extended to 180 s. This suggests that LR is better suited for short-term behavior assessments.

Table 3. Average performance of each machine learning algorithm. The highest score for each technique is marked with an asterisk (*), and the best overall result across all techniques is shown in bold.

		10 s	30 s	60 s	180 s
Accuracy	RF	0.789	0.797*	0.663	0.532
	DT	0.778	**0.821***	0.666	0.505
	XGB	0.776	0.800*	0.600	0.601
	LR	0.775	0.802*	0.600	0.597
Sensitivity	RF	0.682	0.711*	0.659	0.634
	DT	0.744	**0.870***	0.828	0.683
	XGB	0.745	0.700	0.780*	0.669
	LR	0.779*	0.590	0.750	0.683
Specificity	RF	**0.915***	0.899	0.870	0.790
	DT	0.717	0.788*	0.770	0.752
	XGB	0.618	0.690*	0.654	0.610
	LR	0.660	0.670	0.650	0.700*
Precision	RF	0.727	**0.800***	0.785	0.553
	DT	0.746	0.770	0.790*	0.522
	XGB	0.711	0.720*	0.710	0.546
	LR	0.700	0.770*	0.700	0.574

3 Conclusion

Based on the findings presented in this paper, we have successfully explored the utilization of wearable sensors and accelerometer data for detecting cattle behaviors, with a specific focus on feeding and ruminating behaviors. Our study concentrated on in-house cattle, and we collected accelerometer data using collar tags. We employed four machine learning models-RF, XGB, DT, and LR-to classify cattle behavior based on extracted features from the accelerometer data. The results consistently showed that shorter time intervals (10 s and 30 s) yielded better prediction performance across all models, suggesting that analyzing shorter data segments is more relevant for behavior classification. Both RF and DT algorithms demonstrated strong performance across various metrics and time intervals, striking a balance between sensitivity and specificity. XGB and LR also produced competitive results, especially at shorter intervals.

The RF algorithm offers an advantage by being less susceptible to overfitting due to its ensemble approach, which averages results from multiple DTs, reducing model variance and minimizing the risk of poor performance stemming from peculiarities in training and testing data. In contrast, XGB is capable of implicit variable selection and excels in capturing non-linear relationships and high-order interactions between inputs. It efficiently scales with large datasets. However, it is essential to fine-tune XGB parameters carefully, and it may not be the best choice in noisy data conditions due to a higher tendency to overfit compared to RF. Moreover, tuning XGB parameters can be more challenging than RF. Notably, behaviors such as ruminating and feeding serve as crucial indicators for assessing cattle's nutritional intake adequacy. These behaviors can also be influenced by various housing and management strategies, including feed bunk space availability and feed repositioning frequency.

The originality of this paper lies in the approach of feature extraction from accelerometer data, which has proven to be computationally efficient and suitable for real-time analysis of embedded systems. This approach holds potential for application in large-scale livestock management to enhance animal health, welfare, and productivity. Nevertheless, there are certain limitations to this study. The dataset was collected from a specific farm and involved a relatively small number of cattle. To validate the generalizability and robustness of our proposed approach, data from multiple farms and a more extensive cattle population would be advantageous. Additionally, our study specifically focused on in-house cattle, and behavior classification may differ in free-range or pasture-based systems.

In conclusion, this paper provides valuable insights into the application of accelerometer data and machine learning for behavior classification in in-house cattle. These findings carry practical implications for livestock management, precision agriculture, and animal welfare. However, further research is warranted to validate the approach on a larger scale and explore its applicability in various livestock management settings.

References

1. Antanaitis, R., et al.: Change in rumination behavior parameters around calving in cows with subclinical ketosis diagnosed during 30 days after calving. Animals **13** (2023). https://doi.org/10.3390/ani13040595

2. Barwick, J., Lamb, D.W., Dobos, R., Welch, M., Trotter, M.: Categorising sheep activity using a tri-axial accelerometer. Computers and Electronics in Agriculture **145**, 289–297 (2018). https://www.sciencedirect.com/science/article/pii/S0168169917311468

3. Benaissa, S., et al.: On the use of on-cow accelerometers for the classification of behaviours in dairy barns. Res. Veterinary Sci. **125**, 425–433 (2019). https://www.sciencedirect.com/science/article/pii/S003452881730423X

4. Brouwers, S.P., Simmler, M., Savary, P., Scriba, M.F.: Towards a novel method for detecting atypical lying down and standing up behaviors in dairy cows using accelerometers and machine learning. Smart Agric. Technol. **4** (2023). https://doi.org/10.1016/j.atech.2023.100199

5. Cabezas, J., et al.: Analysis of accelerometer and GPS data for cattle behaviour identification and anomalous events detection. Entropy **24** (2022). https://doi.org/10.3390/e24030336

6. Chang, A.Z., Fogarty, E.S., Moraes, L.E., García-Guerra, A., Swain, D.L., Trotter, M.G.: Detection of rumination in cattle using an accelerometer ear-tag: a comparison of analytical methods and individual animal and generic models. Comput. Electron. Agric. **192**, 106595 (2022). https://www.sciencedirect.com/science/article/pii/S0168169921006128

7. Chen, T., Guestrin, C.: XGBoost: a scalable tree boosting system. In: Proceedings of the 22nd ACM SIGKDD International Conference on Knowledge Discovery and Data Mining, pp. 785–794. KDD '16, ACM, New York, NY, USA (2016). https://doi.org/10.1145/2939672.2939785

8. Cox, D.R.: The regression analysis of binary sequences. J. Roy. Stat. Soc.: Ser. B (Methodol.) **20**(2), 215–232 (1958)

9. Ho, T.K.: Random decision forests. In: Proceedings of 3rd international conference on document analysis and recognition, vol. 1, pp. 278–282. IEEE (1995)

10. King, M., LeBlanc, S., Pajor, E., Wright, T., DeVries, T.: Behavior and productivity of cows milked in automated systems before diagnosis of health disorders in early lactation. J. Dairy Sci. **101**(5), 4343–4356 (2018). https://doi.org/10.3168/jds.2017-13686

11. Leliveld, L.M., Riva, E., Mattachini, G., Finzi, A., Lovarelli, D., Provolo, G.: Dairy cow behavior is affected by period, time of day and housing. Animals 12 (2022). https://doi.org/10.3390/ani12040512

12. Montes, M.E., et al.: Relationship between body temperature and behavior of nonpregnant early-lactation dairy cows (2023)

13. Paudyal, S.: Using rumination time to manage health and reproduction in dairy cattle: a review. Vet. Q. **41**, 292–300 (2021). https://doi.org/10.1080/01652176.2021.1987581

14. Turner, L., Udal, M., Larson, B., Shearer, S.: Monitoring cattle behavior and pasture use with GPS and GIS (2000)

15. Weerd, N.D., et al.: Deriving animal behaviour from high-frequency GPS: Tracking cows in open and forested habitat. PLoS ONE 10 (2015). https://doi.org/10.1371/journal.pone.0129030

16. Williams, L.R., Fox, D.R., Bishop-Hurley, G.J., Swain, D.L.: Use of radio frequency identification (RFID) technology to record grazing beef cattle water point use. Comput. Electron. Agric. **156**, 193–202 (2019). https://www.sciencedirect.com/science/article/pii/S0168169918306707

17. Wolhuter, R., Petrus, S., Roux, L., Marais, J., Niesler, T.: Automatic classification of sheep behaviour using 3-axis accelerometer data cough detection view project automatic real-time animal behaviour classification view project automatic classification of sheep behaviour using 3-axis accelerometer data (2014). https://www.researchgate.net/publication/319331093

18. Wu, X., et al.: Top 10 algorithms in data mining. Knowl. Inf. Syst. **14**(1), 1–37 (2008)

LexiFusedNet: A Unified Approach for Imbalanced Short-Text Classification Using Lexicon-Based Feature Extraction, Transfer Learning and One Class Classifiers

Saugata Bose[✉] and Guoxin Su

University of Wollongong, Northfields Ave, Wollongong, Australia
sb632@uowmail.edu.au, guoxin@uow.edu.au

Abstract. The incorporation of lexicon-based feature extraction and the utilization of a one-class classification loss within a transfer learning-based deep neural network offer significant advantages. In lexicon-based feature extraction, weights are assigned to relevant words in short texts, and fine-tuning with these weighted features enables the capture of critical information. Augmenting contextualized word embeddings with lexicon-derived weights highlights the significance of specific words, thereby enriching text comprehension. One-class classification loss methods such as OCSVM or SVDD identify anomalous instances based on word relevance. A comprehensive evaluation on four benchmark datasets has confirmed an improvement in short-text classification performance, effectively addressing issues related to data imbalances, contextual limitations, and noise.

Keywords: Attention mechanism · Lexicon-based Weighted Feature Extraction (LWFE) · Pre-trained language model · Transfer learning · Fine-tuning · One-class Classifier · Short-text · HateBase

1 Introduction

In recent years, research focus on short-text classification has intensified, driven by the proliferation of social media and the demand for personalized recommendation systems. An array of anomalies, including hate speech, cyberbullying, and profanity, pervades this domain [17]. Prior studies have delved into deep learning models [8,12], transfer learning approaches [6,12], and ensemble methods [5,11] to detect such anomalous content. Nevertheless, the unique characteristics of informal text and the challenges posed by imbalanced datasets hinder accurate detection [7,8]. Existing models heavily rely on automatically extracted features and often lack integration of domain-specific knowledge [8,15].

To address these challenges, we propose *LexiFusedNet*, a semi-supervised model that combines a customized approach called "Lexicon-based Weighted

S. Wu et al. (Eds.): PKAW 2023, LNAI 14317, pp. 70–82, 2023.
https://doi.org/10.1007/978-981-99-7855-7_6

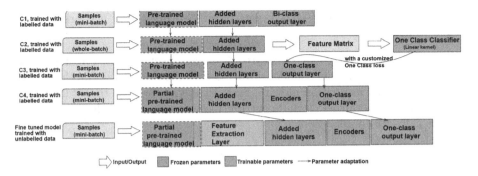

Fig. 1. The fully deep *LexiFusedNet* model consists of multiple steps. In Step 1 and Step 2, parameters are extracted from the base model. In Step 3, another base model is created by modifying the pre-trained language model (PLM) with an added self-attention-based transformer encoder. All three base classifiers are trained using a small-sized labelled dataset. Subsequently, the fine-tuned model, which incorporates a lexicon-based feature extraction layer, is trained using a large unlabelled dataset. To enhance the model's performance, a custom one-class loss function is applied to the one-class output layer. The final output is determined using a custom activation function.

Feature Extraction (LWFE)" transfer learning with BERT, and one-class classifiers (OC-SVM and SVDD). Building upon the "Deep One-Class Fine-Tuning (DOCFT)" model [6], *LexiFusedNet* integrates lexicon-based features with a fine-tuned BERT model and incorporates anomaly detection. Specifically, we focus on detecting hate speech, utilizing a novel feature extraction model called LWFE that incorporates lexicon-based weights derived from the "HateBase" lexicon [20]. These weights capture the degree of hate in short texts and are combined with the BERT model and one-class classifiers. Comparisons with baselines, including word n-grams and continuous bag-of-words vectors, demonstrate the effectiveness of our model. To overcome the scarcity of labelled data, we employ three base classifiers trained on labelled data and fine-tune the model using a large unlabelled dataset, enabling *LexiFusedNet* to adapt to the characteristics of short texts. Furthermore, we experiment with freezing the BERT model and incorporating encoders. Our approach represents the first incorporation of lexicon-based feature weights and one-class classification loss in a fine-tuned deep neural network.

Our main contributions are twofold:

- **Improved Feature Extraction with Deep Neural Network and Attention Mechanism.** We propose "Lexicon-based Weighted Feature Extraction (LWFE)" which dynamically adjusts the relevance and importance of lexical features. Extensive experiments validate its superiority when combined with a deep neural network and attention mechanism.
- **Enhanced Performance with Semi-supervised One-Class Classifiers.** Our enhanced performance surpasses base models by utilizing one-class clas-

sifiers (OC-SVM and SVDD) in our fully deep fine-tuned network trained with unlabelled data.

The remaining sections are structured as follows: Sect. 2 reviews related work, Sect. 3 describes our model and algorithms, Sect. 4 provides details on the experimental setup and evaluation metrics, Sect. 5 analyzes the experimental results, Sect. 6 discusses performance and contributions, and Sect. 7 concludes our work and discusses future directions.

2   Related Work

In recent years, pre-trained neural language models such as [9] and scaled dot-product attention [24] have revolutionized short-text classification. However, they lack domain-specific knowledge. Previous research has demonstrated the value of incorporating manual features and attention mechanisms to capture linguistic information [1]. Inspired by these works, we propose the Lexicon-Weighted Feature Extraction (LWFE) method, which combines lexicon matching and self-attention to focus on essential text segments using lexicon-based weights. Given the presence of imbalanced anomalous data, we treat our LexiFusedNet model as semi-supervised. The MixMatch algorithm [4] and the deep co-training framework [18] have shown the benefits of integrating unlabelled data into semi-supervised learning. Building on this, we employ the LexiFusedNet model as a semi-supervised solution. In the context of short-text anomaly detection, [5] emphasize the limitations of binary classification and underscore the effectiveness of one-class classification [16]. Additionally, [6] demonstrate the power of transfer learning for short-text classification. However, these approaches are developed in a supervised context. To address this, we draw inspiration from [13] to propose a novel semi-supervised deep one-class LexiFusedNet model, leveraging unlabelled data during fine-tuning. Overall, our work incorporates domain-specific knowledge and explores semi-supervised learning, building upon advancements in pre-trained models, attention mechanisms, and one-class classification methods.

3   Fully Deep *LexiFusedNet*

We introduce the *LexiFusedNet* model, which combines transfer learning and lexical features for the classification of anomalous text content. Through the integration of pre-trained models, a self-attention-based transformer, and tailor-made one-class loss functions, we achieve enhanced performance. The final model consists of a partially frozen pre-trained language model (PLM) with additional layers and a customized feature extraction module known as the LWFE. By leveraging a lexicon, our model excels in accurately identifying anomalies in short-text scenarios. Furthermore, we employ unlabelled data to adapt and further enhance performance, especially on imbalanced datasets.

3.1 Building Supervised Pre-trained Models

To construct the *LexiFusedNet* model, we develop a set of multiple base classifiers aimed at capturing distinct aspects of the input data, each contributing to the final predictions. Let us denote the learnable parameters of these base classifiers as $\theta_1, \theta_2, \theta_3, \theta_4$, corresponding to the set of base classifiers $[C1, C2, C3, C4]$. These parameters are subject to updates through an optimization algorithm. The training data for the base classifiers comprise labelled instances $X_l = [x_1, x_2, ..., x_n]$ and their corresponding labels $y = [y_1, y_2, ..., y_n]$.

Base Classifier 1 ($C1$): In $C1$, we estimate the conditional probability distribution $p(y_i = 1|x_i)$ using labelled data, and we obtain the output $z1 = f_1(X; \theta_1)$ from the second-to-last layer. Subsequently, we apply the softmax function in Equation (1) to the preceding layer's output, yielding the projected probabilities $y_{(l)}$, which represent the likelihood of each class.

$$y_{(l)} = \text{softmax}(y_{(l-1)}) = \frac{e^{y_{(l-1)i}}}{\sum_{i=1}^{2} e^{y_{(l-1)i}}} \tag{1}$$

Base Classifier 2 ($C2$): $C2$ is a hybrid one-class model that incorporates anomalous features $\acute{x} \subseteq z1$ from a batch and transfers θ_1 from $C1$. The output of $C2$ is obtained as $z2 = f_2(\acute{x}; \theta_1, \theta_2)$. The optimization objective for $C2$ is defined in Equation (2), encompassing non-negative slack variables ξ penalized within the objective function.

$$\min_{\theta_2, \rho, \xi} \quad \frac{1}{2} \| \theta_2 \|^2 - \rho + \frac{1}{vn} \sum_{i=1}^{n} \xi_i \quad \text{s.t.} \langle \theta_2 \varphi(\acute{x}_i) \rangle \geq \rho - \xi_i, \xi_i \geq 0, \forall i \tag{2}$$

Base Classifier 3 ($C3$): $C3$ is a fully deep One-Class Fine-Tuning (DOCFT) model that integrates a linear kernel-based customized OC-SVM. It introduces a new output layer with weights extracted from the linear OC-SVM of $C2$. The output of $C3$ is denoted as $z3 = f_3(m; \theta_1, \theta_2, \theta_3)$. The model is trained using the optimization objective defined in Equation (3), which incorporates a regularization coefficient λ and updates ρ using minibatch quantile regression.

$$\mathcal{L}(\theta_1, \theta_2, \theta_3, \rho) = \lambda|\theta_1| + \lambda|\theta_2| + \frac{1}{2}|\theta_3|^2 - \rho + \frac{1}{vn} \sum_{i=1}^{n} \max(0, \rho - \langle \theta_3, \varphi_\theta(m_i) \rangle) \tag{3}$$

Base Classifier 4 ($C4$): $C4$ incorporates a self-attention model and a partially pre-trained PLM. The optimization objective for $C4$ is defined in Equation (4), which includes a regularization term and trainable weight vectors. The output of $C4$, denoted as $z4 = f_4(m; \theta_1, \theta_2, \theta_3, \theta_4)$, is achieved through this optimization process.

$$\mathcal{L}(\acute{\theta}, \rho, \theta_4{}^q, \theta_4{}^k, \theta_4{}^v) = \lambda|\acute{\theta}| + f^{\cdot}(\theta_4{}^q, \theta_4{}^k, \theta_4{}^v) +$$

$$\frac{1}{2}|\theta_4|^2 - \rho + \frac{1}{vn} \sum_{i=1}^{n} \max(0, \rho - \langle \theta_4, \varphi_\theta(m_i) \rangle) \tag{4}$$

$$\text{s.t.} \quad \lambda|\acute{\theta}| = \lambda|\theta_1| + \lambda|\theta_2| + \lambda|\theta_3|$$

The *LexiFusedNet* model proficiently classifies anomalous text content by fine-tuning these base classifiers, leveraging transfer learning and lexical features. This approach facilitates the accurate identification of anomalous content in short-text scenarios.

3.2   Building Self-Taught Fine-Tuned One-Class Model

The fine-tuned component of *LexiFusedNet* integrates unlabelled samples X_u and their corresponding features $x_1, x_2, ..., x_m$. This integration involves combining a pre-trained Language Model (PLM) with additional hidden layers and a customized method for incorporating lexical features known as "Lexicon-based Weighted Feature Extraction (LWFE)". Furthermore, it leverages the weights obtained from the fourth base classifier ($C4$).

Mathematically, we represent the weights of the fine-tuned model as $W_{\text{fine-tuned}}$, the transferred weights from $C4$ as θ_4, and the weight transfer operation as $W_{\text{fine-tuned}} = \theta_4$. The expected output of the fine-tuned model is denoted as $Y_{\text{fine-tuned}}$, which can be expressed as: $Y_{fine-tuned} = f(X_u; W_{fine-tuned}) + g(X_u)$

In this equation, the function f processes the input data using the fine-tuned weights, while the function g represents the weighted representation of each word obtained from the LWFE. To train this model effectively and make accurate predictions, a customized one-class loss function is employed. Examples of such loss functions are provided in Equation (4) and Equation (7). These loss functions optimize the parameters $W_{\text{fine-tuned}}$ while considering the integration of lexical features and the fine-tuned weights for precise predictions.

Lexicon-Based Weighted Feature Extraction (LWFE). To incorporate a lexicon of anomalous words into our mathematical model, we begin with a dataset Z comprising n samples denoted as $z_1, z_2, ..., z_n$. We define two sets: T represents the set of m non-anomalous words as $t_1, t_2, ..., t_m$, and U represents the set of p anomalous words as $u_1, u_2, ..., u_p$ obtained from a lexicon. Within this context, let d_1 be the count of anomalous samples in the dataset and d_2 be the count of non-anomalous samples. We employ binary variables to signify the presence of words in the tweets. Specifically, k_{ij} is a binary variable indicating whether the word T_i appears in the tweet Z_j, and v_{ij} is a binary variable indicating whether the word U_j appears in the tweet Z_i.

The calculation of weights for non-anomalous and anomalous words within the tweet documents is outlined as follows:

Weight Calculation for Non-Anomalous Words: For each non-anomalous word T_i in T, we compute the frequency of T_i appearing in the d_1 non-anomalous samples using Equation (5):

$$C_i = \sum k_{ij} \quad \forall (k_{ij}) \in U, z_j \in z_1, z_2, ..., z_{d_1} \tag{5}$$

The weight of each non-anomalous word T_i in the non-anomalous sample set is calculated as $F_i = C_i/d_1$.

Weight Calculation for Anomalous Words: For each anomalous word U_j in U, we determine the frequency of U_j appearing in the d_2 non-anomalous samples using Equation (6):

$$D_j = \sum v_{ij} \quad \forall (v_{ij}) \in T, z_i \in z_{d_1+1}, z_{d_1+2}, ..., z_n \tag{6}$$

The weight of each anomalous word U_j in the anomalous sample set is given by $G_j = D_j/d_2$.

This weight calculation procedure quantifies the presence and significance of specific words in samples categorized as anomalous, enabling us to leverage lexicon-based features to discern correlations between certain words and tweet labels. The final weight vector W_{lex} is formed by concatenating the weight vectors for non-anomalous and anomalous words: $W_{lex} = [F_1, F_2, ..., F_m, G_1, G_2, ..., G_p]$.

This approach allows us to capture the lexical characteristics associated with both non-anomalous and anomalous samples, providing valuable insights for anomaly detection.

Fine Tuning with One-Class Classifiers. Our research explores two variants of one-class classifiers: OC-SVM [21] and SVDD [23]. We introduce a finely tuned deep one-class model that incorporates an output layer, utilizing weights extracted from the $C4$ layer. This model undergoes refinement through training with a substantial set of unlabelled samples.

The learning process of our proposed classifier can be mathematically represented by Equation (4), where the objective is to establish a decision boundary around normal data instances, classifying any data points lying outside this boundary as anomalies. Alternatively, we formulate this learning process as a customized optimization problem. The goal is to discover a hyperplane within the input space that encompasses the normal data points while simultaneously minimizing the volume of the enclosing hypersphere, as illustrated in Equation (7).

$$\mathcal{L}(\acute{\theta}, \rho, \theta_4{}^q, \theta_4{}^k, \theta_4{}^v) = \lambda \|\acute{\theta}\| + f^{\cdot}(\theta_4{}^q, \theta_4{}^k, \theta_4{}^v) +$$

$$\frac{1}{2}\|\theta_4\|^2 + \frac{1}{\nu n}\sum_{i=1}^{m} \max(0, \theta_4^T \varphi_\theta(x_i) - b - R + s_i) \tag{7}$$

$$\text{s.t.} s_i \geq 0 \quad \forall i = 1, 2, \dots m$$

Equation (7) comprises a regularization term, a hinge loss term, and constraints on the slack variables s_i. The hinge loss term quantifies the disparity between the predicted class scores and the desired margin, permitting a certain degree of misclassification within a defined margin.

In summary, our approach optimizes the model by adjusting its parameters and decision boundary conditions to best fit the training data. This results in a decision boundary that effectively distinguishes normal instances from anomalies while allowing for controlled misclassifications within a specific margin.

4   Experimental Setup

The experiment aimed to assess the performance of *LexiFusedNet*, a comprehensive deep learning model that integrates BERT, BiLSTM, Lexical Features, and self-attention-based transformers. We initially trained base classifiers using labelled data, employing various loss functions to optimize their performance. Additionally, we conducted training using unlabelled data to fine-tune the network, showcasing the adaptability and efficacy of the *LexiFusedNet* model in the realm of short-text classification. To achieve optimal results, we utilized the Adam optimizer during the experimentation phase.

4.1   Models

Our model consists of several classifiers trained with labelled data: a binary classifier ($C1$), a hybrid one-class classifier ($C2$), a fully deep fine-tuned one-class classifier model ($C3$), and an encoder-based fully deep fine-tuned one-class anomaly detection classifier ($C4$).

Base Classifiers with Labelled Data. We use a labelled sample set for training. Key details include:

- $C1$ utilizes a small-sized BERT model (*bert-base-uncased*) and is trained as a binary classifier.
- $C2$ employs features from $C1$ and applies an OC-SVM classifier.
- $C3$ adapts parameters from $C1$ and $C2$ and is trained end-to-end using a customized one-class SVM loss function.
- $C4$ fine-tunes higher-level layers of BERT selectively to adapt to detecting anomalous text content while leveraging pre-trained knowledge.

Fine-Tuned Classifiers with Unlabelled Data Via Self-Taught Learning. Our approach leverages the power of Self-Taught Learning, a technique that empowers models to learn from unlabelled data through pseudo-labeling. In this context, we employ the Self-Taught Learning algorithm to fine-tune our *LexiFusedNet* model. This process involves initializing the model with parameters from $C4$, one of our base classifiers, to maintain benchmark performance. Subsequently, we expose *LexiFusedNet* to a vast corpus of unlabelled data, allowing it to adapt and generalize by assigning pseudo-labels to this data. Careful optimization, including hyperparameters like the radius value and learning rate, ensures the model's stability and enhances its anomaly detection capabilities. Self-Taught Learning proves instrumental in evolving our model's proficiency, enabling it to excel in identifying diverse short-text anomalies. This approach is supported by research in self-taught learning methodologies [19].

4.2 Dataset

Labelled Data. The study addresses hate speech detection in short-text content on social media. We utilize four publicly available English hate speech datasets: Davidson (24,802 tweets) [8], StormFront (10,944 posts) [10], SemEval-2019 (10,000 tweets) [2] (focusing on hate speech against immigrants and women in Spanish and English tweets), and HASOC-2019 (5,852 Facebook and Twitter posts) [14].

Unlabelled Data. To address dataset limitations, we incorporate the "US Election Tweets 2020" dataset [3] (439,999 tweets) from Kaggle. This diverse unlabelled dataset reflects short-text anomalies. We preprocess using Table 1 and employ a bag-of-words model for feature extraction (1-gram to 4-grams).

Table 1. Pre-processing Techniques applied on Base models and Fine-Tuned model.

Punctuation, Extra space, Irrelevant characters, Unicode, Stop words, Emoticon, Numbers, URL removal
Tokenization, Infrequent tokens removal (empty tokens or the tokens having one character only.)

4.3 Lexicon

We integrated two lexicon datasets into our LWFE. Firstly, we incorporated the "HateBase" vocabulary dataset [20], encompassing 1,565 keywords categorized by varying degrees of offensiveness. These keywords were treated as indicative of the "hate" category, transcending language nuances.

Secondly, we utilized a n-grams dataset [8], featuring 179 terms from 1-gram to 4-gram combinations. Both lexicon sets enrich our LWFE, enabling the extraction of lexical features for detecting anomalous content.

4.4 Performance Metric

We gauge the *LexiFusedNet* model's performance through essential metrics. The macro-F1 score, which prioritizes the "anomalous" class, assesses overall effectiveness. We minimize false positives and false negatives, following [22] guidelines.

Additionally, we employ the AUC score to evaluate the model's ability to distinguish between target and outlier objects. Higher AUC values indicate superior separation capability. Furthermore, we measure accuracy to determine the percentage of correct *LexiFusedNet* predictions.

5   Result

Table 2 summarizes model performance, including Binary Classifier ($C1$), Hybrid One-Class Classifier ($C2$), Deep One-Class Fine-tuned Model ($C3$), Self-Attention Encoder-Based Deep One-Class Classifier ($C4$), and LexiFusedNet. Evaluation encompasses Davidson, Stormfront, SemEval'19, and HASOC'19 datasets. Remarkably, LexiFusedNet excels in key metrics across datasets. For the Davidson dataset, it achieves the highest macro F1 (0.88), accuracy (0.89), and AUC (0.89), boasting the lowest false positive (0.22) and false negative (0.07) rates. LexiFusedNet maintains its dominance on the Stormfront dataset with macro F1 (0.88), accuracy (0.87), and AUC (0.90), with a slightly elevated FPR (0.28) but low FNR (0.09). SemEval'19 sees LexiFusedNet leading in macro F1 (0.89), accuracy (0.90), and AUC (0.91), while keeping false positives (0.24) and false negatives (0.07) in check. Despite a higher FPR (0.31) and a low FNR (0.20) on the HASOC'19 dataset, LexiFusedNet remains superior in macro F1 (0.69), accuracy (0.73), and AUC (0.74). These results underscore LexiFusedNet's robustness and leadership in short-text classification across diverse datasets.

6   Discussion

Table 2 highlights the superiority of one-class classifier-based models in identifying anomalous short-text, showcasing improvements in macro F1 score (1–6%), accuracy (1–9%), AUC score (1–11%), and reduced FPR and FNR (3–20% and 2–11% respectively).

LexiFusedNet, employing customized Linear OCSVM, achieves notably high macro-F1 scores, excelling on Davidson and Stormfront datasets. SemEval'19 and HASOC'19 datasets also demonstrate its effectiveness. Similarly, *LexiFusedNet* with customized Linear SVDD shows competitive macro-F1 scores (refer Table 3). These results underline our study's contribution, emphasizing enhanced short-text classification performance with one-class classifiers. The inclusion of the Lexicon-based Weighted Feature Extraction (LWFE) contributes to *LexiFusedNet*'s superior performance, with approximately 2–6% higher macro F1 score, improved accuracy (2–9%), and a notable increase in AUC score (2–10%) for the hate class. *LexiFusedNet* effectively reduces the false positive rate (FPR) by 3–20% and the false negative rate (FNR) by 3–15%, minimizing misclassifications. These improvements are attributed to the integration of the lexicon-based weighted features in *LexiFusedNet*.

In contrast to models without the LWFE, *LexiFusedNet* combines lexical features and self-attention-based encoders, accurately capturing the intensity and severity of anomalous text content. Table 4 compares the performance of the LWFE with various base feature sets and lexicons. The module using the "HateBase" lexicon achieves reasonably high macro-F1 scores across all datasets, performing well on the Davidson and SemEval'19 datasets. The n-gram dictionary lexicon-based model shows similar performance. *LexiFusedNet* trained with

Table 2. Presents the performance evaluation of different models: Binary classifier, Hybrid One-Class classifier, Deep One-Class Fine-tuned model, Encoder-Based One-Class Fine-tuned model, and the proposed *LexiFusedNet* model. The performance metrics include macro F1 score, AUC scores of the hate class, accuracy, false positive rate (FPR), and false negative rate (FNR). The evaluations were conducted on the test dataset, and the best results are indicated in bold.

Models	Performance Metric	Davidson	Stormfront	SemEval'19	HASOC'19
Binary Classifier	macro f1	0.82	0.85	0.82	0.62
	Accuracy	0.80	0.83	0.82	0.59
	AUC	0.78	0.81	0.81	0.60
	FPR	0.37	0.35	0.36	0.42
	FNR	0.38	0.23	0.31	0.33
Hybrid One Class Clssifier	macro f1	0.85	0.87	0.83	0.60
	Accuracy	0.81	0.84	0.82	0.64
	AUC	0.83	0.86	0.84	0.65
	FPR	0.36	0.32	0.37	0.40
	FNR	0.36	0.23	0.28	0.31
Deep One Class Fine-tuned model	macro f1	0.85	0.87	0.85	0.61
	Accuracy	0.86	0.89	0.85	0.68
	AUC	0.86	0.90	0.89	0.71
	FPR	0.32	0.31	0.32	0.38
	FNR	0.11	0.15	0.10	0.25
Self-attn Encoder Based Deep One Class Classifier	macro f1	0.86	0.86	0.88	0.65
	Accuracy	0.86	**0.89**	0.88	0.69
	AUC	0.86	**0.92**	0.89	0.72
	FPR	0.26	**0.28**	0.29	0.35
	FNR	0.10	0.10	0.09	0.22
LexiFusedNet	macro f1	**0.88**	**0.88**	**0.89**	**0.69**
	Accuracy	**0.89**	0.87	**0.90**	**0.73**
	AUC	**0.89**	0.90	**0.91**	**0.74**
	FPR	**0.22**	**0.28**	**0.24**	**0.31**
	FNR	**0.07**	**0.09**	**0.07**	**0.20**

different feature sets achieves competitive scores but slightly lower than *LexiFusedNet* with the LWFE supporting the claim of improved feature extraction.

Table 3. Presents the macro-f1 performance of *LexiFusedNet* with various one-class implementation- customized OC-SVM and customized linear SVDD. The evaluations were conducted on the test dataset, and the best results are indicated in bold.

Models	Davidson	Stormfront	SemEval'19	HASOC'19
LexiFusedNet trained with customized Linear OCSVM	**0.88**	**0.88**	**0.89**	0.67
LexiFusedNet trained with customized Linear SVDD	0.84	0.84	0.86	**0.69**

Table 4. Provides a comparison of macro-F1 performance evaluation for the "Lexicon-based Weighted Feature Extraction (LWFE)" across various base feature sets (n-gram feature, BOW feature, word embedding feature). It also presents the performance of the LWFE using the "Hatebase" lexicon and a curated lexicon. The evaluations were conducted on the test dataset, with the best results highlighted in bold.

Models	Davidson	Stormfront	SemEval'19	HASOC'19
LexiFusedNet trained with LWFE using "HateBase" Lexicon	**0.88**	**0.88**	**0.89**	**0.69**
LexiFusedNet trained with LWFE using "n-gram dict" Lexicon	**0.88**	0.86	0.88	0.67
LexiFusedNet trained with bag-of-words feature	0.85	0.85	0.86	0.64
LexiFusedNet trained with 1-gram feature	0.85	0.84	0.87	0.64
LexiFusedNet trained with 2-gram feature	0.85	0.85	0.87	0.64
LexiFusedNet trained with 3-gram feature	0.86	0.86	0.87	0.65
LexiFusedNet trained with 4-gram feature	0.87	0.86	0.88	0.66
LexiFusedNet trained with BERT embedding feature	0.85	0.86	0.86	0.65

7   Conclusion

The integration of "Lexicon-based Weighted Feature Extraction (LWFE)" into *LexiFusedNet* significantly enhances its ability to detect anomalies in short-text data from social media. This approach effectively addresses data imbalance issues and utilizes unlabeled data to boost performance. Through the combination of lexicon-based features and self-attention-based encoders, the model gains a deeper understanding of the context surrounding anomalous text, resulting in improved accuracy. Key contributions of this approach include the utilization of one-class classifiers, outperforming binary classifiers, and the integration of lexicon-based features for enhanced detection accuracy. *LexiFusedNet* consistently demonstrates robust performance across various datasets, making it a pioneering advancement in the realm of short-text classification.

References

1. Basiri, M.E., Nemati, S., Abdar, M., Cambria, E., Acharya, U.R.: ABCDM: an attention-based bidirectional CNN-RNN deep model for sentiment analysis. J. Future Gener. Comput. Syst. **115**, 279–294 (2021)
2. Basile, V., Bosco, C., Fersini, E., Nozza, D., Patti, V., Rangel, F., Rosso, P., Sanguinetti, M.: Semeval- 2019 task 5: multilingual detection of hate speech against immigrants and women in twitter. In: Proceedings of the 13th International Workshop on Semantic Evaluation, pp. 54–63. Association for Computational Linguistics, Minneapolis, Minnesota, USA (2019)
3. Bauyrjan. 2020 US election Tweets-Unlabeled. https://www.kaggle.com/datasets/bauyrjanj/2020-us-election-tweets-unlabeled (2020)
4. Berthelot, D., Carlini, N., Goodfellow, I., Papernot, N., Oliver, A., Raffel, C.: MixMatch: a holistic approach to semi-supervised learning. In: 33rd Conference on Neural Information Processing Systems. NeurIPS, Vancouver, Canada (2019)
5. Bose, S., Su, G.: Deep one-class hate speech detection model. In: Proceedings of the Thirteenth Language Resources and Evaluation Conference. ELRA, Marseille, France, pp. 7040–7048 (2022)
6. Bose, S., Su, G., Liu, L.: Deep one-class fine-tuning for imbalanced short text classification in transfer learning. In: Accepted for International Conference on Advanced Data Mining and Applications. ADMA, Shenyang, China (2023)
7. Chalapathy, R., Chawla, S.: Deep learning for anomaly detection: a survey. arXiv preprint arXiv:1901.03407 [cs.LG] (2019)
8. Davidson, T., Warmsley, D., Macy, M., Weber, I.: Automated hate speech detection and the problem of offensive language. arXiv preprint arXiv:1703.04009 [cs.CL] (2017)
9. Devlin, J., Chang, M., Lee, K., Toutanova, K.: Bert: pre-training of deep bidirectional transformers for language understanding. In: Proceedings of NAACL-HLT 2019, pp. 4171–4186. Association for Computational Linguistics, Minneapolis, Minnesota (2019)
10. Gibert, O., Perez, N., García-Pablos, A., Cuadros, M.: Hate speech dataset from a white supremacy forum. In: Proceedings of the ALW2, pp. 11–20. Association for Computational Linguistics, Brussels, Belgium (2018)
11. Kulkarni, A., Hengle, A., Udyawar, R.: An attention ensemble approach for efficient text classification of indian languages. In: Proceedings of the 17th International Conference on Natural Language Processing (ICON): TechDOfication 2020 Shared Task, pp. 40–46. NLP Association of India (NLPAI) (2020)
12. Li, Q., et al.: A survey on text classification: from traditional to deep learning. ACM Trans. Intell. Syst. Technol. **13**(2), 1–41 (2022)
13. Li, W., Guo, Q., Elka, C.: A positive and unlabeled learning algorithm for one-class classification of remote-sensing data. IEEE Trans. Geosci. Remote **49**(2), 717–725 (2011)

14. Mandl, T., Modha, S., Majumder, P., Patel, D., Dave, M., Mandlia, C., Patel, A.: Overview of the HASOC track at FIRE 2019: hate speech and offensive content identification in Indo-European languages. In: Proceedings of the FIRE '19, pp. 14–17. Association for Computing Machinery, New York, NY, USA (2019)

15. Mathew, B., Saha, P., Yimam, S.M., Biemann, C., Goyal, P., Mukherjee, A.: HateXplain: a benchmark dataset for explainable hate speech detection. arXiv preprint arXiv:2012.10289 [cs.CL] (2022)

16. Moya, M. M., Koch, M. W., Hostetler, L. D.: One-class classifier networks for target recognition applications. https://www.osti.gov/biblio/6755553. Accessed 8 Apr 2023

17. Poletto, F., Basile, V., Sanguinetti, M., Bosco, C., Patti, V.: Resources and benchmark corpora for hate speech detection: a systematic review. Lang. Resour. Eval. **55**(2), 477–523 (2020)

18. Qiao, S., Shen, W., Zhang, Z., Wang, B., Yuille, A.: Deep co-training for semi-supervised image recognition. In: Ferrari, V., Hebert, M., Sminchisescu, C., Weiss, Y. (eds.) ECCV 2018. LNCS, vol. 11219, pp. 142–159. Springer, Cham (2018). https://doi.org/10.1007/978-3-030-01267-0_9

19. Raina, R., Battle, A., Lee, H., Packer, B., Ng, A.Y.: Self-taught learning: transfer learning from unlabeled data. In: Proceedings of the 24th International Conference on Machine Learning, pp. 759–766. Association for Computing Machinery, Corvalis, Oregon, USA (2007)

20. https://hatebase.org/ . Accessed 16 Jun 2023

21. Schölkopf, B., Alexander, J. S.: Support Vector Machines, Regularization, Optimization, and Beyond. MIT Press, pp 656–657 (2002)

22. Tax, D. M. J.: Data description toolbox. https://homepage.tudelft.nl/n9d04/. Accessed 8 Apr 2023

23. Tax, D.M.J., Duin, R.P.W.: Support vector data description. Mach. Learn. **54**(1), 45–66 (2004)

24. Vaswani, A., et al.: Attention is all you need. In: 31st Conference on Neural Information Processing Systems (NIPS 2017). Long Beach, CA, USA (2017)

Information Gerrymandering in Elections

Xiaoxue Liu[1,2], Shohei Kato[2(✉)], Fenghui Ren[1], Guoxin Su[1], Minjie Zhang[1], and Wen Gu[3]

[1] School of Computing and Information Technology, University of Wollongong, Wollongong, Australia
`xl018@uowmail.edu.au`, {`fren,guoxin,minjie`}`@uow.edu.au`
[2] Department of Computer Science and Engineering, Nagoya Institute of Technology, Nagoya, Japan
`shohey@nitech.ac.jp`
[3] Center for Innovative Distance Education and Research, Japan Advanced Institute of Science and Technology, Ishikawa, Japan
`wgu@jaist.ac.jp`

Abstract. When making decisions, individuals often seek advice from their family, friends, and social network connections. In this way, individuals' opinions are susceptible to influence from their connections' viewpoints. For example, in elections, individuals may initially support one party, while social influence may sway their choice to another. A recent study by Stewart et al. introduced a metric, *influence assortment*, to quantify the phenomenon of information gerrymandering that one party can influence more voters from other parties by strategically distributing their members among the social networks. While this metric correlates strongly with voting outcomes, the finding is only suitable for two-party elections. In this paper, we define the influence assortment that incorporates the level of similarity (homophily) among neighbours in the social network and extend it to multi-party elections. We examine its ability to predict voting outcomes when all parties initially have equal votes and average degrees. Through simulations using a stochastic model of voting behaviour, we demonstrate that the correlation between the influence gap and vote difference is a strong predictor in both small and large scale-free networks.

Keywords: Social Choice · Information Gerrymandering · Voting

1 Introduction

In today's digital societies, social media has become an increasingly important source of information for individuals. Consequently, their opinions may be vulnerable to being influenced by information flow which may be constrained by these social networks. The study of how social networks affects collective decision-making has attracted a large amount of attention, including the study of majority dynamics [2], stabilization [9], termination [5], or manipulation [6]

S. Wu et al. (Eds.): PKAW 2023, LNAI 14317, pp. 83–97, 2023.
https://doi.org/10.1007/978-981-99-7855-7_7

of opinion diffusion. In the multi-agent system community, the study of social choice in social networks becomes an active research topic [12]. Researchers in this area focused on studying the computational complexity of manipulating collective decision-making outcomes via social influence [10,19], adding edges [14] or removing edges [8].

Following this line of research, Stewart et al. [16] conducted a voter game in a Nature paper to explore how the structure of the influence network affects collective decision-making. They discovered a phenomenon called "information gerrymandering," where the topology of the influence network can bias the vote outcome in favour of a particular party, even when both parties are of equal size. This occurs when one party effectively distributes its influence in social networks to sway individuals from the opposing party, without wasting influence on those already convinced. To capture this phenomenon, they introduced a static graph-theoretic metric called "influence assortment." Through experiments involving human subjects and simulations, they found that a party with a higher influence assortment more frequently achieves a winning consensus compared to the other party. In other words, the asymmetric influence assortment, which they called influence gap, can skew the final vote in favour of a specific party, demonstrating its potential to predict voting outcomes. Later, Bara et al. [3] examined the influence gap metric in graphs with a community structure and replicated its predictive power, even when confronted with various initial partisan majorities.

The metric influence gap enables us to sidestep the computing equilibrium of a highly complex system where individuals change their opinions repeatedly. It provides a novel way to simplify the analysis of opinion diffusion dynamics, which is a notably complex problem [5,9]. Moreover, it allows us to understand the effect of manipulation deeply, for example, via strategically arranging the position of a party's member to change the network dynamics.

The results presented in [3,16] are subject to several limiting assumptions. Firstly, the existing definition of influence assortment fails to account for the presence of homophily. It overlooks the scenario where voters from a party form an echo chamber, leading to an inflated value for influence assortment that does not accurately reflect the effectiveness of a party's influence distribution. Secondly, the metric of influence gap is specifically tailored for two-party elections and cannot be directly applied to measure information gerrymandering in multi-party elections. This paper aims to address these limitations by revising the definition of influence assortment to better capture the phenomenon of information gerrymandering in more diverse scenarios. We propose a new definition of influence assortment that incorporates the homophily factor and accommodates more than two parties. Furthermore, we utilize this revised metric to predict election outcomes in situations where parties are of equal size.

The contributions of this paper are twofold. 1. We propose a new definition of influence assortment that improves its accuracy in representing the effectiveness of a party's distributed influence in social networks. Furthermore, we extend this concept to encompass multi-party elections, enabling a better understanding and measurement of information gerrymandering in various scenarios.

2. We investigate the predictive capabilities of the newly devised influence assortment in multi-party elections, when each party has an equal size and an equal number of influencers. Through simulating elections, we demonstrate a significant correlation between the difference in influence assortment and the difference in votes, indicating the potential for the metric to predict voting outcomes effectively.

The remainder of the paper is structured as follows. We introduce related works in Sect. 2. In Sect. 3, we explain information gerrymandering. In Sect. 4, we define influence assortment that incorporates a homophily factor and extend it to multi-party elections. In Sect. 5, we presents the experiment and results. In Sect. 6 we conclude our paper.

2   Related Works

Voting in social networks has been widely studied [8, 10–12, 14, 19], and many of them are explored from the aspect of computational complexity. For example, Wilder et al. [19] initiated a problem of election control via social influence, where a third party tried to find a seed of nodes in social networks to spread messages on or against a target candidate such that the election outcome was altered in its favor. To model the amount of influence in a more fine-grained way, a linear threshold ranking model was proposed in a follow-up work by Corò et al. [10]. Similarly, according to Faliszewski et al. [11], bribery with opinion diffusion in networks based on majority dynamics is computationally hard when a node – a cluster of like-minded voters – adopts the majority view of its neighborhood. Other works include investigating how to add edges [14] or remove edges [8] to alter election outcomes.

However, the above works treat social networks as external intervention, such as by spreading messages or adding edges and all concentrate on election control; while our paper and papers in [13, 17] view networks a source of information for voters to make decisions. But the focus of them are different. Liu et al. [13] analyzed the utilitarian social welfare under different strategic voting behaviors. Tsang and Larson [17] addressed the strategic behaviour affected by the average degree of networks. Unlike them, our purpose is to investigate how the topology of networks (or placements of each party's node) can be used as a tool to predict voting outcomes.

A close research avenue concerns the computational models of opinion diffusion [5–7, 9], where agents' opinions are influenced by messages spread across the social network. Works in this area mainly focus on simple two-opinion settings, including the study of stabilizing opinion diffusion [9], when it would be terminated [5] and manipulating the result of opinion diffusion [6]. In addition, complex opinions over some issues, modelled as structural preferences such as ordinal rankings, were also considered [7]. We consider a similar complex form of opinions where voters have a rank list of m parties and are likely to update their votes based on opinions from their neighbors in the social network and models of voting behaviors. Our purpose is to explore whether a graph-theoretic metric, MIG, can correlate with voting outcomes in multi-party elections.

3   Preliminaries

Here we consider elections, where n voters are split into m parties. Voters are allowed to change their voting intentions successively based on a stochastic voting behaviours model [16], in reaction to aggregated polling information. The aggregated polling data is determined by the position of their neighbors in a graph, called an influence network. Now we will introduce the definition of an election and an influence network.

Definition 1 (Election). An election $En = (\mathcal{P}, V, T)$ consists of:

- $\mathcal{P} = \{\mathcal{G}, \mathcal{B}, \mathcal{R}, \cdots, \mathcal{C}\}$, a set of finite parties, where $|\mathcal{P}| = m \geq 2$.
- $V = \{v_1, \cdots, v_n\}$, a set of n voters. Voters are associated with a particular party by a function, $p : V \to \mathcal{P}$. For example, $p(i) = \mathcal{G}$ represents the party of voter v_i is $\mathcal{G}$.
- $T > \frac{1}{m}$ is a threshold to decide a single winner in the election. The number of votes for a party, such as party $\mathcal{G}$, is denoted as $M(\mathcal{G}) = |\{v_i \in V \mid p(i) = \mathcal{G}\}|$. Party $\mathcal{G}$ wins if it has the largest vote share $M(\mathcal{G})/n$ and this share surpasses the threshold T, while other parties lose. A deadlock occurs if no party meets this requirement.

Definition 2 (Influence network). An influence network is defined as a directed graph $G = (V, E)$, consisting of

- $V = \{v_1, \ldots, v_n\}$, a set of nodes. Each node represent a voter.
- $E \subset V \times V$, a set of edges representing connections among voters. For a vertex v_i, a local 'poll' consists of its direct neighbourhood $N^+(i) = \{v_j \mid (v_i, v_j) \in E\} \cup \{v_i\}$. The $poll$ represents voting intentions of v_i's neighbourhood, denoted as $\Delta_i = \{\Delta_{i,\mathcal{G}}, \Delta_{i,\mathcal{B}}, \Delta_{i,\mathcal{R}}, \cdots, \Delta_{i,\mathcal{C}}\}$, where $\Delta_{i,\mathcal{G}} = \frac{|\{v_j \in N^+(i) \mid p(j) = \mathcal{G}\}|}{|N^+(i)|}$ is the fraction of voters voting for party $\mathcal{G}$. Let $p(N_i^+) = |\{p(i) \mid v_i \in N^+(i)\}|$ denote the number of parties that receives votes in the neighbourhood $N^+(i)$.

3.1   Information Gerrymandering from Literature

Information Gerrymandering in Two-Party Elections: Information gerrymandering refers to the phenomenon that the topology of an influence network can surprisingly influence the voting outcomes. Specifically, a party can flip a large number of voters from other parties and receive votes whose number exceeds their proportion if they assort influence more effectively than the other parties across the influence network. This phenomenon is recovered by Stewart et al. [16] from extensive social network experiments with human subjects via a voter game. Furthermore, they found that real-world collective decisions with two parties also bear the hallmarks of information gerrymandering, such as in European legislative bodies and between Democrats and Republicans.

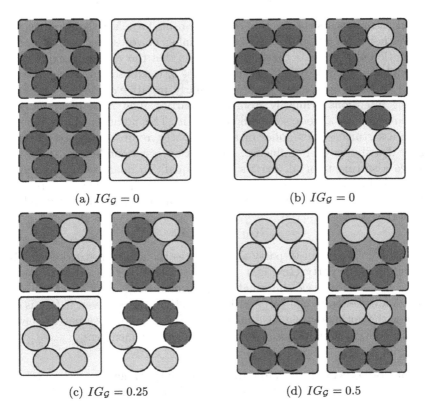

(a) $IG_\mathcal{G} = 0$ (b) $IG_\mathcal{G} = 0$

(c) $IG_\mathcal{G} = 0.25$ (d) $IG_\mathcal{G} = 0.5$

Fig. 1. Influence assortment and information gerrymandering in two-party elections. The local information available to a voter is determined by their position in a directed network. **a-d**: each example consists of 4 complete graphs, among which nodes, represented by circles, have identical in-degree and out-degree of 5. The colour, or line style, of a node indicates the assigned party to a voter, and the background colour, or line style of the rectangle's edge, indicates the corresponding party with the majority of influence on each node (no rectangle's edges indicate no majority influence). **a**: $A_\mathcal{G} = A_\mathcal{B} = 1$, **b**: $A_\mathcal{G} = A_\mathcal{B} = 0.39$. **a-b**, when both parties have the same distribution of influence assortment across their members. **c**: $A_\mathcal{G} = 0.5$, $A_\mathcal{B} = 0.25$, **d**: $A_\mathcal{G} = 2/3$, $A_\mathcal{B} = 1/6$. **c-d**, asymmetric assortment where the party $\mathcal{G}$ distributes their influence more effectively.

To capture the presence of information gerrymandering in two-party elections, a metric of *influence assortment* on a node level a_i and a party level $\mathcal{A}_\mathcal{G}$ were defined by Stewart et al. [16] as follows:

$$a_i = \begin{cases} \Delta_{p(i)} & \Delta_{p(i)} \geq \frac{1}{2} \\ -(1 - \Delta_{p(i)}) & \Delta_{p(i)} < \frac{1}{2} \end{cases}, \quad \Delta_{p(i)} = \frac{|\{v_j \in N^+(i)|p(j) = p(i)\}|}{|N^+(i)|} \quad (1)$$

$$\mathcal{A}_\mathcal{G} = \frac{\sum_{p(i)=\mathcal{G}} a_i}{M(\mathcal{G})} \quad (2)$$

where $\Delta_{p(i)}$ represents the fraction of voters voting for v_i's assigned party in v_i's neighbourhood $N^+(i)$, and $M(\mathcal{G})$ is the number of votes received by party $\mathcal{G}$. The notation a_i represents the voting intention that the voter v_i is exposed to in their neighbourhood $N^+(i)$. Positive a_i means v_i is exposed to voting intentions primarily from its own assigned party. Similarly, negative a_i means v_i is exposed to voting intentions primarily from other parties. The value of a_i represents how homogeneous a node's neighbourhood is. The notation $\mathcal{A}_\mathcal{G}$ is the mean of node assortments over nodes of a single party, representing how effectively a party distributes their influence. Information gerrymandering occurs if the influence assortment for all parties is not equal. To quantify the information gerrymandering, the concept of *influence gap* for two-party elections is defined as the difference of influence assortment by Stewart et al. [16] using the following in equations:

$$IG_\mathcal{G} = A_\mathcal{G} - A_\mathcal{B}. \tag{3}$$

If $\mathcal{A}_\mathcal{G}$ is greater than 0, party $\mathcal{G}$ distributes their influence more effectively than the opposite party (In Fig. 1 (c-d), the values of $IG_\mathcal{G}$ are 0.25 and 0.5, respectively). In this case, information gerrymandering occurs and the voting outcomes are skewed to the party with the positive $\mathcal{A}_\mathcal{G}$. However, if $IG_\mathcal{G}$ is equal to 0, then the voting outcome is unbiased (In Fig. 1 (a-b), both parties have the same distribution of influence assortment across their members).

Information Gerrymandering in Multi-party Elections: Bara et al. [4] extend the influence assortment (Eq. 1) to multi-party elections as follows:

$$a_i = \begin{cases} \Delta_{p(i)} & p(i) = \arg\max_{\mathcal{C} \in \mathcal{P}} \Delta_{i,\mathcal{C}} \\ -\max_{\mathcal{C} \in \mathcal{P}} \Delta_{i,\mathcal{C}} & \text{otherwise} \end{cases} \tag{4}$$

Based the above extension, $A_\mathcal{G}$ is greater than $A_\mathcal{R}$ in the example influence network with three parties (Fig. 2). However, this extension fails to accurately reflect the fact that party $\mathcal{R}$ exerts the majority of influence on voters within two complete graphs (depicted as two rectangles with a pink background).

4   Effective Influence Assortment in General Scenarios

Although the difference of influence assortment in [16] can measure the information gerrymandering, the definition of influence assortment on the party level fails to represent how effectively a party distributes their influence. For example, the influence assortment $\mathcal{A}_\mathcal{G} = 1$ is greater in Fig. 1 (a) than that ($\mathcal{A}_\mathcal{G} = 2/3$) in Fig. 1 (d), however, in the former, party $\mathcal{G}$ cannot influence any nodes from party $\mathcal{B}$ while in the latter, party $\mathcal{G}$ can probably influence as many as 6 nodes from $\mathcal{B}$. Additionally, this definition only suits two-party elections, which cannot handle elections with more than two parties.

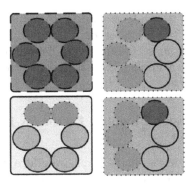

Fig. 2. Influence assortment and information gerrymandering in multi-party elections. Each rectangle consists of a complete graph with 6 circles, or nodes. The colour, or line style, of a node indicates the assigned party to a voter, and the background colour, or line style of the rectangle's edge, indicates the corresponding party with the majority of influence on each node. Based on Eq. 4, $A_\mathcal{R} = 0.208$, $A_\mathcal{G} = 0.625$, and $A_\mathcal{B} = 0.083$. This definition cannot quantify gerrymandered party $\mathcal{R}$ because $A_\mathcal{R} < A_\mathcal{G}$ means party $\mathcal{G}$ can affect more members from other parties than party $\mathcal{R}$.

4.1   Influence Assortment on the Node Level

Considering for multi-party elections, we define the influence assortment as the difference in force of social influence between a voter's assigned party and the other strongest rival:

$$a_i = f(\Delta_{p(i)}) - f(\max_{\mathcal{C} \neq p(i), \mathcal{C} \in \mathcal{P}} \Delta_{i,\mathcal{C}}) \qquad (5)$$

$$f(\Delta_{p(i)}) = \Delta_{p(i)} \frac{exp[h(\Delta_{p(i)} - \frac{1}{m})]}{1 + exp[h(\Delta_{p(i)} - \frac{1}{m})]}, \ h > 0 \qquad (6)$$

Equation 5 follows the original definition of influence assortment by Stewart et al., i.e., $a_i = f(\Delta_{p(i)}) - f(1 - \Delta_{p(i)})$, as presented in Supplementary Information Sect. 3 [16]. However, we subtract $f(\max_{\mathcal{C} \neq p(i), \mathcal{C} \in \mathcal{P}} \Delta_{i,\mathcal{C}})$ due to the assumption that voters primarily concern themselves with the influence from the most promising opponent in multi-party elections. Similarly, the sign of a_i indicates whether v_i's party constitutes the majority party, while the value represents the intensity of that party's influence assorting in its neighbourhood. This definition can be reduced to the original version for two-party elections.

Non-linearity in the "pull" Function f: In Eq. 5, f is an increasing function that represents the resulting "pull" of the aggregated social influence from a party on nodes. Equation 6 follows the definition of $f(\Delta_{p(i)}) = \Delta_{p(i)} \frac{exp[h(\Delta_{p(i)} - \frac{1}{2})]}{1 + exp[h(\Delta_{p(i)} - \frac{1}{2})]}$ in [16]. The sigmoid function here accounts for the non-linearity of $\Delta_{p(i)}$. It captures the idea that a party with $1/m$ of influence exerts a disproportionate pull on the nodes because such influence suggests the party's potential as a winner in the neighborhood. Naturally, this definition can be reduced to two-party elections. Parameter h determines the degree of non-linearity. A high value of h implies that a voter is strongly "pulled" towards the party when $\Delta_{p(i)} > 1/m$.

4.2   Considering the Echo Chamber Factor for Influence Assortment on the Party Level

For influence assortment on the party level, we add a weight to the influence assortment on each voter. This weight reflect how effectively the voter can influence members from other parties. Equation 7 represents the average influence assortment of a party, where $g(|p(N^+(i)| - 1)$ accounts for the weight for the voter v_i. If all the members in v_i's neighbourhood are from one party, these nodes form an echo chamber. In this case, voter v_i is ineffectively positioned, and the party wastes their influence on those who are already convinced. In contrast, if a party distributes their influence in the neighbourhood with different party members, it is assumed to be more effective as the party can persuade members from other parties to flip their votes. Hence, a weight $g(|p(N^+(i)| - 1)$ (damping factor) should be added considering the level of voters' homophily for the overall influence assortment on the party level. For simplification, we consider a simple function of g:

$$A_{\mathcal{G}} = \frac{\sum_{p(i)=\mathcal{G}} g(|p(N^+(i)| - 1)a_i}{M(\mathcal{G})} \tag{7}$$

$$g(|p(N^+(i)| - 1) = |p(N^+(i)| - 1, \tag{8}$$

where $g(|p(N^+(i)| - 1)$ is the number of other parties in the neighbourhood. For instance, in Fig. 1 (a), each party assortment is zero when a damping factor of 0 is multiplied by the influence assortment on each node.

4.3   Influence Gap

Equation 9 represents the influence gap of party $\mathcal{G}$ over other parties. Similarly, the sign of influence gap represents whether party $\mathcal{G}$ distributes their influence the most effectively, while the value is the strength of this gap.

$$IG_{\mathcal{G}} = A_{\mathcal{G}} - \max_{C \neq B} A_C. \tag{9}$$

Example 1. Now we take the example of an influence network of Fig. 2 to show how to calculate the influence assortment for a party. Based on Eq. 5, 6, 7, and 8, $A_{\mathcal{R}} = (2 * [f(\frac{1}{2}) - f(\frac{1}{3})] * 6 + [f(\frac{1}{3}) - f(\frac{2}{3})] * 2)/8 = [6f(\frac{1}{2}) - 5f(\frac{1}{3}) - f(\frac{2}{3})]/4$. Similarly, $A_{\mathcal{G}} = [f(\frac{1}{6}) - 2f(\frac{1}{3})]/4$ and $A_{\mathcal{B}} = [f(\frac{2}{3}) + f(\frac{1}{3}) - 2f(\frac{1}{2})]/2$. It is obvious that $IG_{\mathcal{R}}$ is the maximal among the three parties. In addition, the $IG_{\mathcal{G}}$ in Fig. 1 (d) is greater than that in Fig. 1 (a), which shows party $\mathcal{G}$ distributes their influence more effectively in the former than in the latter.

5 Experiments

In this section, we specify the optimal value of h in Eq. 6 to best capture the impact of information gerrymandering, whereby an influence gap favours one party. Subsequently, we assess the predictive capabilities of the influence gap in multi-party elections. We compare the influence gap values obtained before the elections and the voting outcomes resulting from simulated selections. In the simulations, voters update their voting intentions based on a stochastic model of voting behaviours which have been validated through social experiments involving human subjects in [16].

5.1 The Behavioural Model

To study information gerrymandering, Stewart et al. [16] conducted a 240-second voter game. Each play was initially assigned to a party. During the game, players continuously adjusted their voting intentions based on local polls. After the game, players received different payoffs: a higher payoff if their assigned party won (with a vote ratio above a super-majority threshold $T > 0.5$), a lower payoff if they lost, or the lowest payoff if a dead lock occurred (neither party reached the $T > 0.5$ threshold).

Backed by social experiments with human subjects, Stewart et al. [16] developed a stochastic model of voting behaviours. The model depends on two factors: the game phase and the players' perception of the game's outcome. Each voter votes for their assigned party using six probability parameters, denoted as $pro^{k,l}$, where k represents the game phase (early, late), l represents how voters projected the results (win, lose, deadloack). Table 1 displays the empirical distribution of these six probabilities.

Table 1. The empirical probability distribution [16].

early win	early deadlock	early lose	late win	late deadlock	late lose
0.0169	0	0.2098	0.0092	0.055	0.2822
0	0.0042	0.0747	0.0031	0.0048	0.0644
0	0.0021	0.046	0	0.0096	0.0153
0	0.0042	0.0402	0.0031	0.0024	0.0215
0.0028	0.0042	0.0172	0	0.0096	0.0337
0	0.0104	0.0345	0.0031	0.0048	0.0031
0.0085	0.0125	0.0259	0.0061	0.0048	0.0337
0.0056	0.0125	0.0287	0	0.0144	0.0429
0	0.0375	0.0402	0.0092	0.0191	0.0307
0.0169	0.0354	0.0575	0.0123	0.0263	0.1429
0.9493	**0.8771**	**0.4253**	**0.954**	**0.8493**	**0.3296**

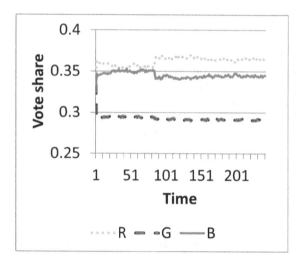

Fig. 3. results of a three-party election under the behavioural model on the influence network in Fig. 2.

We extend the voter model to accommodate three or more parties. A party wins if it gains the highest number of votes and reaches the threshold $\mathcal{T} > 1/m$, while other parties lose. Deadlocks occur when none of party surpasses the threshold $\mathcal{T}$ or when multiple parties reach the threshold with the same number of votes. Each voter v_i votes for the assigned party based on the same set of six probability probabilities $pro_i^{k,l}$. In contrast, the voter votes for the party with the highest $\Delta_{i,c}$ with a probability $1 - pro_i^{k,l}$. Figure 3 presents the vote share of the three parties using the stochastic voter model within the influence network 2. Note that the game does not guarantee convergence as it terminates after 240 s.

5.2   Experiment 1: Specifying the Non-linearity Parameter h

In this experiment, we specify the parameter h of f in Eq. 6 by correlating each party's influence gap and the resulting vote difference from the simulation. Voters' strategies of the 6 probabilities are sampled from the empirical distribution in Fig. 3 (a). The vote difference for party $\mathcal{R}$ is $\mathcal{R}$'s average vote share minus the highest average vote share among the other parties $(\mathcal{R})$ exclusive.

Construct Small Influence Networks: Firstly, we construct influence networks consisting of 4 complete graphs, each with 6 nodes. These 24 nodes, divided into three equal-sized parties (8 voters per party) have five incoming and outgoing edges each. Party $\mathcal{R}$ has an advantage in persuading voters while the other parties waste much of their influence. To create such influence networks, we employ the method for constructing electoral gerrymandering [16]. Electoral gerrymandering involves drawing voting districts so that one party wins an imbalanced number of seats [15]. To do so, the gerrymandered party's voters are clustered in some districts and connected sparsely in others. Specifically, we generate four complete sub-graphs with six nodes, as shown in Fig. 4. These sub-graphs are initially isolated, with party $\mathcal{R}$ effectively distributing their influence. Subsequently, we merge these four isolated graphs by randomly rewiring pairs of edges with the same party assignment but from different sub-graphs, repeating this process 10^4 times.

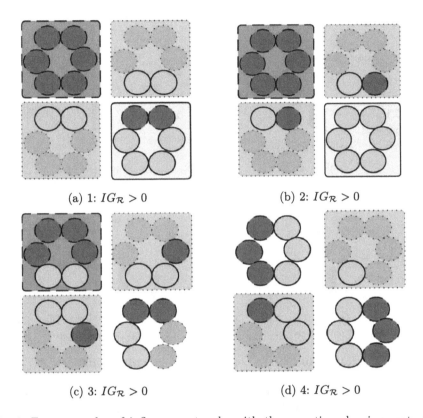

(a) 1: $IG_\mathcal{R} > 0$ (b) 2: $IG_\mathcal{R} > 0$

(c) 3: $IG_\mathcal{R} > 0$ (d) 4: $IG_\mathcal{R} > 0$

Fig. 4. Four examples of influence networks with three parties, showing party $\mathcal{R}$'s advantage in persuading voters. Similar to Fig. 1, each example consists of 4 complete graphs, among which nodes, represented by circles, have identical in-degree and out-degree of 5. The colour, or line style, of a node indicates the assigned party to a voter, and the background colour, or line style of the rectangle's edge, indicates the corresponding party with the majority of influence on each node (no rectangle's edges indicate no majority influence).

Results: We simulate the behavioural model on the listed four influence networks depicted in Fig. 4. The correlation between the influence gap and vote difference for various values of h in the definition of influence assortment is presented in Fig. 5. Other influence networks generate similar results, which are not shown here due to space limitations. Our analysis reveals that the linear function f, when $h = 0$, can yield a small influence gap and account for some variation in the resulting vote difference. However, as h increases, the impact becomes much more pronounced, indicating that the resulting definition of influence assortment and influence gap serve as strong predictors of the resulting vote difference. Therefore, we select $h = 100$ for the calculation of influence assortment in the subsequent experiment.

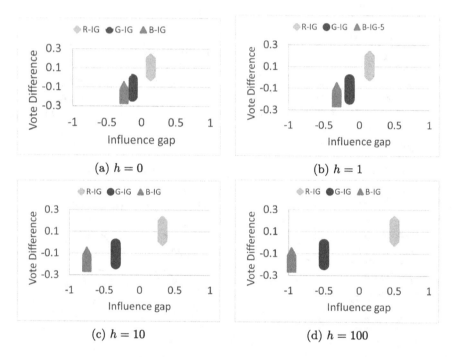

Fig. 5. Influence gap and vote difference for different values of h in the definition of influence assortment for influence network 3. The resulting definition of influence assortment and influence gap is a good predictor of resulting vote difference. When h becomes greater, the correlation between the influence gap and vote difference becomes stronger.

5.3 Experiment 2: Examine the Predictive Power of Influence Gap in Scale-Free Networks

We examine the usage of the influence gap in larger networks consisting of 120 voters, equally divided into 3 parties, with each party having the same average degree. We analyze the statistical correlation between the influence gap before elections and the resulting difference in vote shares after conducting simulations.

Construct Scale-Free Influence Networks: Many human-generated networks, such as the Internet, exhibit a property of scale-free where there are a few highly connected hubs and numerous sparsely connected nodes. To generate such networks, we employ the Barabási-Albert (BA) random model [1]. In our setting, we start with a complete graph of n_0 (set to 9) nodes and use an attachment parameter of d (set to 8). New nodes are added one at a time and connected with d existing vertices with the probability proportional to their current degrees. In real-life social networks, individuals typically connect with others who share some similarities. To incorporate this, we introduce levels of homophily between nodes. We multiply the probability of connecting node v_i to v_j with a homophily factor $0 < homophily \leq 1$, if both nodes' are from the same party. This way of generating homophilic Barabási-Albert graphs is also used in [18]. The generated graph is referred to as the HBA graph.

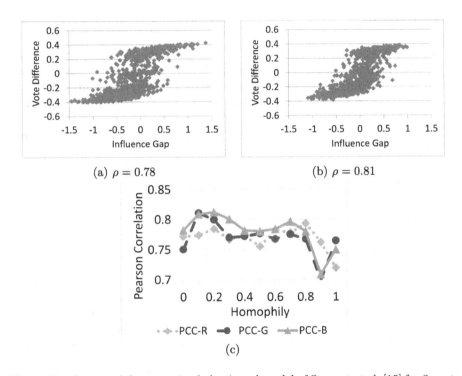

Fig. 6. Simulations of the extension behavioural model of Stewart et al. [15] for 3-party elections. In (H)BA graphs the influence gap correlates relatively strongly with vote difference, having a Pearson's correlation $\rho \approx 0.8$, and passing a significance test with $p < 10^7$. a: BA graphs. b:HBA graphs with homophily factor 0.3. c: Homophilic factor are varied with *homophliy* $= 0$ being the BA graph. The homophily factor does not have too much influence on the Pearson correlation because the influence gap is close in this way of generating influence networks.

Results: Figure 6 (a) and (b) show the Pearson Correlation between the influence gap and vote difference. While the correlation between the influence gap and vote difference is around 0.8, the metric of influence gap provides insights into predicting the voting outcomes when parties are highly competitive with the same initial number of votes and the same average degree. The advantage of using the influence gap metric lies in its simplicity and ease of computation, as it only requires knowledge of the influence network's structure. Unlike other approaches, there is no need to obtain exact parameters of the 6 probabilities for all voters or engage in time-consuming simulations of the election process. Additionally, Fig. 6 (c) depicts the changes in the Pearson Correlation as the homophily factor varies. The correlation value is quite stable as the homophily factor increases because the average influence gap is close and small. This value is less than 0.2 in (H)BA influence network when parties are equal-sized.

6 Conclusion

We have defined influence assortment that can effectively quantify the phenomenon of information gerrymandering with both two-party and multi-party elections. This revised definition extends its applicability to a broader range of scenarios. We evaluated the predictive power of this concept, by simulating elections using a stochastic behavioural model. Our experimental results demonstrate that the influence gap serves as a strong predictor in highly competitive scenarios where parties have an equal number of voters. Moreover, it is important to further validate the impact of information gerrymandering in multi-party elections through social experiments involving human subjects.

References

1. Albert, R., Barabási, A.L.: Statistical mechanics of complex networks. Rev. Mod. Phys. **74**(1), 47 (2002)
2. Auletta, V., Ferraioli, D., Greco, G.: Reasoning about consensus when opinions diffuse through majority dynamics. In: Proceedings of the Twenty-Seventh International Joint Conference on Artificial Intelligence (IJCAI), pp. 49–55 (2018)
3. Bara, J., Lev, O., Turrini, P.: Predicting voting outcomes in presence of communities. In: Proceedings of the 20th International Conference on Autonomous Agents and MultiAgent Systems, pp. 151–159 (2021)
4. Bara, J., Lev, O., Turrini, P.: Predicting voting outcomes in the presence of communities, echo chambers and multiple parties. vol. 312 (2022). https://doi.org/10.1016/j.artint.2022.103773
5. Botan, S., Grandi, U., Perrussel, L.: Proposition wise opinion diffusion with constraints. In: Proceedings of the 4th AAMAS Workshop on Exploring Beyond the Worst Case in Computational Social Choice (EXPLORE) (2017)
6. Bredereck, R., Elkind, E.: Manipulating opinion diffusion in social networks. In: Proceedings of the Twenty-Sixth International Joint Conference on Artificial Intelligence (IJCAI), pp. 894–900 (2017)

7. Brill, M., Elkind, E., Endriss, U., Grandi, U., et al.: Pairwise diffusion of preference rankings in social networks. In: Proceedings of the Twenty-Fifth International Joint Conference on Artificial Intelligence (IJCAI), pp. 130–136 (2016)
8. Castiglioni, M., Ferraioli, D., Gatti, N.: Election control in social networks via edge addition or removal. In: Proceedings of the AAAI Conference on Artificial Intelligence. vol. 34, pp. 1878–1885 (2020)
9. Christoff, Z., Grossi, D.: Stability in binary opinion diffusion. In: Baltag, A., Seligman, J., Yamada, T. (eds.) LORI 2017. LNCS, vol. 10455, pp. 166–180. Springer, Heidelberg (2017). https://doi.org/10.1007/978-3-662-55665-8_12
10. Corò, F., Cruciani, E., D'Angelo, G., Ponziani, S.: Exploiting social influence to control elections based on scoring rules. In: IJCAI 2019: the 28th International Joint Conference on Artificial Intelligence, Macao, China, 10–16 August 2019, pp. 201–2017. AAAI Press/IJCAI (2019)
11. Faliszewski, P., Gonen, R., Koutecký, M., Talmon, N.: Opinion diffusion and campaigning on society graphs. In: Proceedings of the 27th International Joint Conference on Artificial Intelligence, pp. 219–225 (2018)
12. Grandi, U.: Social choice and social networks. In: Trends in Computational Social Choice, pp. 169–184 (2017)
13. Liu, X., Ren, F., Su, G., Zhang, M.: Strategies improve social welfare: an empirical study of strategic voting in social networks. In: Long, G., Yu, X., Wang, S. (eds.) AI 2022. LNCS (LNAI), vol. 13151, pp. 203–215. Springer, Cham (2022). https://doi.org/10.1007/978-3-030-97546-3_17
14. Sina, S., Hazon, N., Hassidim, A., Kraus, S.: Adapting the social network to affect elections. In: Proceedings of the 2015 International Conference on Autonomous Agents and Multiagent Systems, pp. 705–713 (2015)
15. Stephanopoulos, N.O., McGhee, E.M.: Partisan gerrymandering and the efficiency gap. The University of Chicago Law Review, pp. 831–900 (2015)
16. Stewart, A.J., Mosleh, M., Diakonova, M., Arechar, A.A., Rand, D.G., Plotkin, J.B.: Information gerrymandering and undemocratic decisions. Nature **573**(7772), 117–121 (2019)
17. Tsang, A., Larson, K.: The echo chamber: strategic voting and homophily in social networks. In: Proceedings of the 2016 International Conference on Autonomous Agents & Multiagent Systems, pp. 368–375 (2016)
18. Tsang, A., Salehi-Abari, A., Larson, K.: Boundedly rational voters in large (r) networks. In: Proceedings of the 17th International Conference on Autonomous Agents and Multi Agent Systems, pp. 301–308 (2018)
19. Wilder, B., Vorobeychik, Y.: Controlling elections through social influence. In: International Conference on Autonomous Agents and Multiagent Systems (2018)

An Assessment of the Influence of Interaction and Recommendation Approaches on the Formation of Information Filter Bubbles

Zihan Yuan[1], Weihua Li[2], and Quan Bai[1](✉)

[1] University of Tasmania, Hobart, Australia
{zyuan0,quan.bai}@utas.edu.au
[2] Auckland University of Technology, Auckland, New Zealand
weihua.li@aut.ac.nz

Abstract. AI-based recommendation approaches can contribute to the formation of ideological isolation, reinforcing users' existing beliefs and limiting exposure to diverse perspectives. Additionally, different Human-Computer Interaction (HCI) approaches may have varying impacts on the diversity of users' information consumption as well. This study focuses on three HCI approaches, namely Search, Click and Scroll, with users exclusively engaging in one approach throughout the experiment. Four recommendation strategies, including Random, Collaborative Filtering, Content-based Filtering, and Keyword-based Matching, are implemented and evaluated. The experimental results reveal that although all three HCI approaches exacerbate the filter bubble effect, a strategically designed combination of certain recommendation algorithms and HCI approaches has the potential to promote a more diverse and balanced online information environment.

Keywords: Recommendation algorithm · Filter bubble effect · Human-Computer Interaction approach

1 Introduction

The rapid growth of Internet users has led to the emergence of AI-based systems as a means to retain and engage users, thereby promoting user stickiness [16]. Personalized recommendation algorithms have significantly enhanced the online experience by tailoring content to individual preferences, such as related search results and product recommendations. Despite their benefits, the filter bubble effect has emerged as a critical concern highlighted by researchers [7,12]. The filter bubble effect characterizes the tendency of online personalization to reinforce users' existing preferences and biases, resulting in narrowed perspectives and hindering their openness to new viewpoints. Analogous to overfitting in machine learning, where models fit training data excessively, the filter bubble effect restricts individuals' willingness to accept new perspectives, eventually leading to ideological isolation (i.e., filter bubbles) [11].

S. Wu et al. (Eds.): PKAW 2023, LNAI 14317, pp. 98–110, 2023.
https://doi.org/10.1007/978-981-99-7855-7_8

In real-world applications, the integration of recommendation algorithms with diverse HCI approaches plays a vital role in enhancing online user experiences. As shown in Fig. 1, the lifeline of user interaction with the recommendation system includes various components. It begins with inputs from the user, such as personal information, queries, and ratings of items. The system then generates outputs in the form of recommended topic lists and information about each topic. The effectiveness of the interaction is further influenced by the HCI design elements, including factors such as the number of topics displayed at a time and the layout of the interface [13].

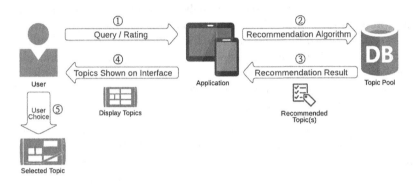

Fig. 1. User interaction with recommendation system.

These recommendation algorithms embedded applications provide various services, which encompass search, click, scroll, etc. Each HCI approach elicits distinct user behaviors, characterized by differences in purposefulness, time taken to locate content, and timing of user interest. Notably, the purposefulness of users navigating the system differs, in descending order, between search, click, and scroll functionalities. Search functionality exhibits the highest purposefulness, with users actively seeking specific content. Click functionality requires users to make decisions among multiple options, potentially without a strong inclination towards a particular topic. In contrast, when users interact with the system through scroll functionality, they passively consume content without making explicit choices, as they remain uncertain about the upcoming content. Moreover, the time required to locate specific content follows the same order, with searching being the most time-consuming and scrolling being the least demanding. Additionally, the timing of user interest varies across these functionalities. Users searching for a topic exhibit strong initial preferences before delving into the search results, while users engaging in click functionality already possess prior knowledge of the topic and then decide to explore its content further after reading the title. Conversely, users interacting with the system through scroll functionality only ascertain their interest after fully or partially consuming the content. It is crucial to acknowledge that different recommendation algorithms contribute differently to the formation of filter bubbles, and it remains essential to determine how users' interaction with the system through different HCI approaches impacts the diversity of information consumption.

In this paper, we aim to examine the contribution of different HCI approaches to information diversity and the formation of filter bubbles. To achieve this aim, we simulate three real-world functionalities associated with their corresponding HCI approaches, search, click and scroll. Considering the interplay between recommendation algorithms and HCI approaches, each functionality is investigated under various recommendation algorithms, including Collaborative Filtering (CF), Content-based Filtering (CB), and Keyword-based Matching (KB). Furthermore, we investigate how different combinations of recommendation algorithms and HCI approaches impact the belief diversity of users. As each functionality presents information in a distinct manner, characterized by differences in the width and depth of knowledge, we anticipate that they will lead to variations in users' knowledge and opinion diversity. We hypothesize that different functionalities will uniquely contribute to the formation of filter bubbles due to their influence on the patterns of user information consumption.

The key contributions of this paper can be categorized into two aspects.

- This study examines how different HCI approaches impact users' openness to new viewpoints, which underscores the importance of fostering an online environment that is rich in diverse perspectives, thus contributing positively to the broader information ecosystem.
- This study investigates the interplay between recommendation algorithms and HCI approaches, and how these interactions collectively shape user belief diversity. It provides valuable insights with the potential to mitigate the filter bubble effect and promote a more diverse and balanced online information environment.

The rest of this paper is organized as follows. In Sect. 2, we review the related works in AI-based recommendation systems from an HCI perspective, the impact of recommendation algorithms on the formation of filter bubbles, and the measurement of the filter bubble effect. Section 3 introduces the preliminaries of this study and the formal definitions of some related concepts. In Sect. 4, we discuss the simulation-based experimental setup and analyze the experimental results. Finally, Sect. 5 concludes the paper and outlines potential directions for future work.

2   Related Works

In this section, we review the related studies that explored the recommendation algorithm embedded HCI approaches, the contribution of recommendation algorithms to the formation of filter bubbles, and the measurement of the filter bubble effect.

Conventional preference-based recommendation algorithms prioritize user interests and preferences. CF provides recommendations based on similar users' preferences [15], while CB recommends items based on item attributes [6]. These distinct algorithms for generating recommendations can influence the formation of filter bubbles and the resulting impact on users' exposure to diverse viewpoints and perspectives. Although recommendation algorithms improve users' online experiences, they can inadvertently exacerbate the filter bubble effect by restricting users' exposure to diverse viewpoints [4,14]. Lunardi et al. [10] propose a metric to quantify filter bubbles in news recommendations, assessing homogeneity levels as an indicator, with higher homogenization suggesting a greater tendency towards the formation of filter bubbles. They conclude that CF algorithms contributed to polarization due to the overlapping of topic content. Similarly, Bechmann and Nielbo [1] examine the filtering of ideologically similar content by recommendation algorithms on social media platforms. They utilize link source analysis and content semantics analysis to evaluate information similarity within non-overlapping content segments. Their findings indicate that the filter bubble effect affected 10–27.8% of users, which increases with higher thresholds for identifying overlapping content segments. Likewise, Flaxman et al. [5] investigate the impact of online information consumption on ideological isolation. Their research emphasizes the association between social media platforms and web search engines with ideological segregation, which can contribute to the formation of filter bubbles. They conclude that recommendation algorithms play a vital role in influencing users' information consumption patterns and contributing to their ideological isolation. Bryant et al. [2] examine the bias exhibited by preference-based recommendation algorithms, specifically highlighting the YouTube algorithm's tendency to favor right-leaning political videos, including those promoting racist views. Their findings suggest that preference-based recommendation algorithms can reinforce users' biases. Also, it is evident that these algorithms contribute differently to the formation of filter bubbles. Hu et al. [8] conduct simulations to explore the formation of filter bubbles and find that CB algorithms have more impact on isolating individuals from diverse information compared to CF algorithms.

Besides the quality of recommendation algorithms, Swearingen and Rashmi [13] emphasize the significance of user interaction with recommendation systems from an HCI perspective. They highlight that the effectiveness of a recommendation system relies on HCI factors that shape users' interactions with the system. For instance, the number of items presented at a time will influence the time needed for the user to make a choice, details of recommended items (e.g., title and image) can attract the user's interest before they engage in the recommendation results, and information on other users' ratings inspires trust in the system. Valdez et al. [3] also suggest that the ultimate effectiveness of recommendation systems should go beyond the accuracy of algorithms, and focus on the HCI-related aspects that affect the user experience when interacting with the systems. They underscore the need for transparency in system logic to recommend items and the explainability of recommendation results to enhance user satisfaction.

While existing research primarily focuses on the influence of various algorithms on the formation of filter bubbles and enhancing user acceptance of recommendations, limited attention has been given to the role of different HCI approaches adopted by real-world applications in the formation of filter bubbles. To address this gap, our study aims to investigate the impact of various HCI approaches on users' information consumption and the formation of filter bubbles.

3 Preliminaries

In this section, we present a comprehensive overview of the key concepts and terminology necessary to understand the subsequent discussions and analysis in this paper, including formal definitions, HCI approaches, recommendation strategies, and the measurement of the filter bubble effect.

3.1 Formal Definitions

A recommendation system $S = \langle U, A, T \rangle$ encompasses the components necessary for generating topic recommendations within an AI-based platform. The system is composed of a set of n users $U = \{u_1, u_2, ..., u_n\}$, a set of m available topics for recommendation $T = \{T_1, T_2, ..., T_m\}$, and an AI platform A, which utilizes its algorithms to facilitate the recommendation of a specific topic $T_i \in T$ to a particular user $u_j \in U$.

Definition 1. A User, denoted as $u_i \in U$, represents an individual entity within the user base of the recommendation system. Each user possesses distinctive beliefs, which shape their interaction with the system. Users' beliefs are not static but rather dynamic, susceptible to change over time through their engagement with the recommended topics, which will be explained in Definition 3.

Definition 2. A Topic, denoted as $T_i \in T$, represents a specific subject or area of interest within the recommendation system. Topics serve as fundamental units for recommendation algorithms to provide personalized recommendation services. Each topic encompasses a distinct group of items that share a common major content, allowing the system to organize and present recommendations to users. Each item belongs to and only belongs to exactly one topic. It is important to note that different users may possess varying beliefs in the topics, reflecting their individual interests and preferences within the system.

Definition 3. User Belief, denoted as $b_i^x \in (0, 1)$, quantifies the degree to which a user u_i expresses interests towards items within the topic T_x. The value of b_i^x ranges from 0 to 1, indicating a spectrum of user attitudes. As b_i^x approaches 0, the user exhibits a negative attitude or disinterest towards the topic T_x, while approaching 1 signifies a positive attitude or favorability towards T_x. A value of $b_i^x = 0.5$ indicates a neutral attitude, suggesting an absence of strong belief towards or against T_x. It is important to note that user beliefs are dynamic and subject to change as a result of user interaction with the recommendation system. Furthermore, the sum of a user's beliefs for all topics must equal 1, ensuring a comprehensive representation of their beliefs within the system.

Table 1 shows a sample user belief of two users u_1 and u_2 towards each of five topics $T = \{T_1, T_2, ..., T_5\}$.

Table 1. Sample user belief.

	T_1	T_2	T_3	T_4	T_5
u_1	0.217	0.296	0.201	0.235	0.051
u_2	0.012	0.356	0.402	0.011	0.219

Definition 4. User Similarity quantifies the similarity between two users, u_i and u_j, which is denoted as $sim(u_i, u_j)$. It is a measure formulated based on their beliefs, b_i and b_j, towards each topic within the recommendation system. User similarity assesses the degree of resemblance in user preferences and interests, which is formulated as:

$$sim(u_i, u_j) = \frac{b_i b_j^T}{\|b_i\| \cdot \|b_j\|}, \tag{1}$$

where b_i and b_j represent the user beliefs of u_i and u_j concerning each topic.

Table 2 shows a sample user similarity of three users u_1, u_2 and u_3 based on their topic preferences.

Table 2. Sample user similarity.

	u_1	u_2	u_3
u_1	1.	0.891	0.623
u_2	0.891	1.	0.774
u_3	0.623	0.774	1.

Definition 5. Topic Correlation, denoted as $\rho(T_x, T_y) \in [0, 1]$, quantifies the degree of association between two topics T_x and T_y within the recommendation system. A value of $\rho(T_x, T_y) = 0$ indicates a lack of relevance between T_x and T_y, implying that they have minimal impact on each other. Conversely, as $\rho(T_x, T_y)$ approaches 1, the correlation between T_x and T_y strengthens, suggesting a higher likelihood of potential influence. In the context of our recommendation system,

topic correlation measures the potential impact between different topics. Specifically, when $\rho(T_x, T_y)$ is close to 1, it signifies a strong correlation between T_x and T_y, indicating that the user's acceptance of T_x is likely to influence their acceptance of its highly related topic T_y.

Table 3 shows a sample topic correlation of five topics $T = \{T_1, T_2, ..., T_5\}$.

Table 3. Sample topic correlation.

	T_1	T_2	T_3	T_4	T_5
T_1	1.	0.316	0.184	0.205	0.568
T_2	0.316	1.	0.653	0.749	0.654
T_3	0.184	0.653	1.	0.106	0.299
T_4	0.205	0.749	0.106	1.	0.724
T_5	0.568	0.654	0.299	0.724	1.

Definition 6. Topic Consumption, denoted as $c_{i,t}^x \in (0, 1]$, quantifies the degree of user engagement and consumption with topic T_x at timestamp t. A higher value of $c_{i,t}^x$ indicates a greater degree of consumption by user u_i on topic T_x at timestamp t. As users interact with the recommendation system, their beliefs may evolve over time, reflecting new interests or shifting priorities. The degree of user consumption on a particular topic plays a crucial role in shaping these beliefs. The more users engage with and consume content within a specific topic, the stronger their belief towards that topic becomes.

3.2   HCI Approaches

HCI approaches encompass the various ways in which users interact with the system to explore and consume recommended topics. In this study, we focus on three primary modes of interaction, i.e., Search, Click, and Scroll.

Search. When users engage in the Search functionality, they actively initiate a search query by inputting specific keywords or phrases to explore a particular topic of interest within the system. The system then responds by generating a list of recommended topics that closely match the search query. Users are presented with these search results and subsequently choose one topic from the provided list based on their individual beliefs. If a user possesses limited prior knowledge or awareness of a specific topic, they may not initiate a search query related to that topic.

Click. Click functionality involves users selecting and clicking on a specific topic from a set of recommended options presented by the system. Users make a conscious decision to explore a particular topic among the available recommendations, which is typically driven by users' existing knowledge or partial interest in the topic. This approach signifies a level of user engagement and active involvement, as users express their intention to further investigate the content associated with the selected topic.

Scroll. Scroll functionality refers to users passively navigating through the presented topic one by one without actively making explicit choices. It is characterized by users relying on the system to deliver a curated stream of items, without the need for immediate decision-making or active selection. During scroll functionality, users are automatically presented with a continuous flow of content, allowing them to explore a variety of topics without committing to any specific choice at that moment.

3.3 Recommendation Strategies

There are many AI-based recommendation strategies available, which can be categorized as user-based CF, CB, KB, etc. In this study, we specifically implement our experiment under four prominent recommendation strategies:

Random (RD): RD provides recommendations randomly. This strategy without AI-recommendation works as the baseline in the experiment.

Collaborative Filtering (CF): CF uses the similarity between a user and other users as a weight to provide recommendations. The utility of recommending topic T_x to a user u_i is formulated as:

$$score_{CF}(u_i, T_x) = \sum_{j=1}^{m} sim(u_i, u_j) \cdot b_j^x, \tag{2}$$

where m denotes the number of users in the user base, and $sim(\cdot)$ denotes the similarity between two users u_i and u_j.

Content-Based Filtering (CB): CB uses the topic correlation between all the topics as a weight to provide recommendations. The utility of recommending topic T_x to a user u_i is formulated as:

$$score_{CB}(u_i, T_x) = \sum_{y=1}^{n} \rho(T_x, T_y) \cdot b_i^y, \tag{3}$$

where n denotes the number of topics within the recommendation system.

Keyword-Based Matching (KB): KB is only applied for the Search functionality, in which the user actively searches for a specific topic, then KB recommends topics based on the ranking of topic correlation associated with that particular topic.

3.4 Filter Bubble Measurement

As defined in Definition 3, each user $u_i \in U$ possesses a distinctive belief matrix, which describes their beliefs $b_i^x \in (0,1)$ towards each topic. To quantify the diversity of user's beliefs, we employ the concept of entropy to assess the level of diversity within the recommendation system [9]. Specifically, a user u_i's belief in a topic T_x can be interpreted as the probability of their engagement with content within T_x, with stronger beliefs corresponding to higher consumption probabilities. To capture the extent of variability and dispersion in users' preferences, the belief diversity of user u_i at timestamp t is formulated as:

$$BD_{i,t} = -\sum_{k=1}^{n} b_{i,t}^k \ln(b_{i,t}^k), \tag{4}$$

where n signifies the number of topics within the recommendation system, and $b_{i,t}^x$ represents the user's belief for each individual topic at timestamp t.

Therefore, a higher value of belief diversity $BD_{i,t}$ signifies a greater diversity of beliefs held by a user u_i at timestamp t. In turn, a lower belief diversity value implies a higher probability of u_i being influenced by the filter bubble effect, as their beliefs are more concentrated and less diverse.

4 Experiments

4.1 Experimental Settings

We conduct the experiments from two directions, recommendation algorithms and HCI approaches. The experiments involve simulating an application with a user base of 50 users and a topic pool of 100 topics. User beliefs b_i^x and topic correlations $\rho(T_x, T_y)$ are randomly initialized, where $b_i^x \in (0,1)$ and $\rho(T_x, T_y) \in [0,1]$. To analyze the formation of filter bubbles, three users, User 13, User 14 and User 46, are randomly selected from the user base for examination. The assumptions of experiments are as follows:

- For each simulation, the user only engages with one type of HCI approach at all timestamps.
- Starting from timestamp 0, each user consumes and only consumes one topic T_x at each timestamp. Following the user's consumption of a specific topic, their beliefs are updated based on the chosen topic T_x.
- For both Search and Click functionalities, when a user u_i selects a particular topic T_x, they fully consume the content within that topic (i.e., $c_i^x = 1$). In the case of Scroll functionality, where users are passively exposed to content, the extent to which the users have engaged with the content is considered. The value of topic consumption $c_i^x \in (0,1]$ is simulated based on the user's current beliefs in T_x.

4.2 Results and Discussion

Experiment 1: Recommendation Algorithms Analysis. The experiment focuses on investigating the influence of different recommendation algorithms on user belief diversity. Through a comparison of figures for the same functionality, it can be observed that the performance of the same algorithm remains consistent across different users. These experimental findings highlight how users' engagement in Search, Click, and Scroll functionalities can influence the evolution of their beliefs and the resulting diversity or narrowness of their belief systems.

Simulation of Recommendations in *Search* Functionality. Search Functionality is simulated using the KB algorithm, with the RD algorithm serving as the baseline. The results, illustrated in Fig. 2, reveal that both algorithms contribute to a decrease in users' belief diversity within a short period. This demonstrates that even without AI recommendations, users' beliefs still become narrow as a result of engaging in Search functionality. Despite this, the KB algorithm contributes to a narrower user belief compared to the RD algorithm, indicating a more focused information consumption. This pattern suggests that users who actively search for a specific topic tend to possess pre-existing preferences in this topic, and thus are more likely to reinforce their existing beliefs.

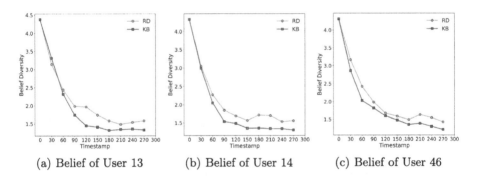

(a) Belief of User 13   (b) Belief of User 14   (c) Belief of User 46

Fig. 2. Search functionality: Filter bubble formation.

Simulation of Recommendations in *Click* Functionality. Click Functionality is simulated using the CF and CB algorithms, with the RD algorithm as the baseline. Figure 3 presents the results, showing that the RD algorithm leads to the most diverse user belief, followed by the CB algorithm. In contrast, the CF algorithm exhibits a more pronounced contribution to ideological isolation, resulting in the narrowest user belief.

Simulation of Recommendations in *Scroll* Functionality. Scroll Functionality is simulated using the CF and CB algorithms, with the RD algorithm as the baseline. The results are demonstrated in Fig. 4. The RD algorithm exhibits minor fluctuations in users' belief diversity over time, indicating a relatively

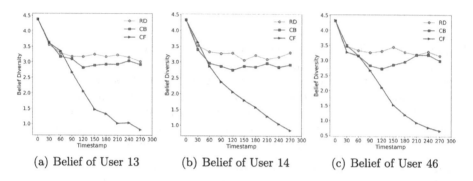

Fig. 3. Click functionality: Filter bubble formation.

stable level of belief diversity. On the other hand, both the CF and CB algorithms display a declining trend in users' belief diversity, with the CF algorithm rapidly converging to an extremely low value within a short period, while the CB algorithm exhibits significant fluctuations over time.

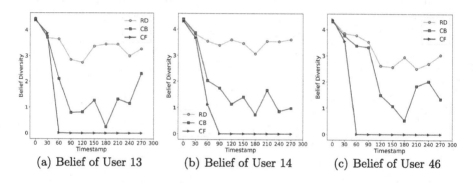

Fig. 4. Scroll functionality: Filter bubble formation.

Experiment 2: AI-Based HCI Approaches Analysis. The experiment focuses on the interaction between recommendation algorithms and HCI approaches, specifically emphasizing their collective influence on user belief diversity. The experiment involves five combinations, namely Search + KB, Click + CB, Click + CF, Scroll + CB, and Scroll + CF.

The findings, as shown in Fig. 5, reveal a consistency in the performance of specific recommendation algorithm and HCI approach pairings when applied to different users. In particular, Click + CB contributes to the most diverse user beliefs, offering a promising avenue for enhancing belief diversity. Conversely, Scroll + CF tends to promote narrower user beliefs, emphasizing the potential consequences of such a combination. Scroll + CB exhibits significant fluctuations in belief diversity over time, signifying its impact in maintaining a dynamic information consumption. Intriguingly, Search + KB initially leads to narrower user beliefs compared to Click + CF in the short term but transitions to fostering more diverse user beliefs in the long term. These findings enhance our understanding of how recommendation algorithm and HCI approach pairings can impact the formation of filter bubbles within AI-based recommendation systems.

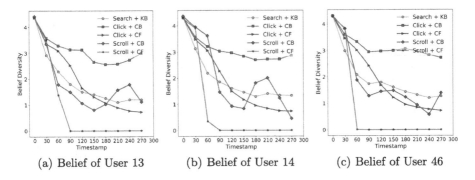

(a) Belief of User 13   (b) Belief of User 14   (c) Belief of User 46

Fig. 5. Combinations of recommendation algorithm and HCI approach.

5   Conclusion and Future Work

This study investigates the influence of three HCI approaches on users' belief diversity within AI-based recommendation systems. The experimental results demonstrate a consistent algorithm performance across different users engaging in the same functionality. The findings indicate that users' beliefs tend to become narrower, even in the absence of AI recommendations, due to their pre-existing preferences. The AI-based recommendation algorithms amplify this effect, leading to a further narrowing of user beliefs compared to the baseline RD algorithm. Moreover, strategically aligning recommendation algorithms with HCI approaches in the design of AI-based recommendation systems possesses the potential to decelerate the formation of filter bubbles when compared with alternative combinations. As a result, recommendation strategies can be thoughtfully designed to mitigate the potential negative consequences of filter bubbles.

Further work can focus on the investigation of how other HCI elements (e.g., the number of topics presented for Search and Click functionality) can impact the diversity of users' information consumption. In addition, real-world datasets can be adopted in future works to develop approaches that foster a broader exposure to diverse perspectives.

References

1. Bechmann, A., Nielbo, K.L.: Are we exposed to the same "news" in the news feed? Digit. J. **6**(8), 990–1002 (2018)
2. Bryant, L.V.: The YouTube algorithm and the alt-right filter bubble. Open Inf. Sci. **4**(1), 85–90 (2020)
3. Calero Valdez, A., Ziefle, M., Verbert, K.: HCI for recommender systems: the past, the present and the future. In: Proceedings of the 10th ACM Conference on Recommender Systems (RecSys 2016), pp. 123–126. Association for Computing Machinery, New York, NY, USA (2016). https://doi.org/10.1145/2959100.2959158
4. Fernandes, M.R.: Confirmation bias in social networks. Math. Soc. Sci. **123**, 59–76 (2023)
5. Flaxman, S., Goel, S., Rao, J.M.: Filter bubbles, echo chambers, and online news consumption. Public Opin. Q. **80**(S1), 298–320 (2016)
6. Guo, Q., Sun, Z., Zhang, J., Theng, Y.L.: An attentional recurrent neural network for personalized next location recommendation. In: Proceedings of the AAAI Conference on artificial intelligence. vol. 34, pp. 83–90 (2020)
7. Haim, M., Graefe, A., Brosius, H.B.: Burst of the filter bubble? Effects of personalization on the diversity of google news. Digit. J. **6**(3), 330–343 (2018)
8. Hu, Y., Wu, S., Jiang, C., Li, W., Bai, Q., Roehrer, E.: AI facilitated isolations? The impact of recommendation-based influence diffusion in human society. In: Proceedings of the 31st International Joint Conference on Artificial Intelligence, pp. 5080–5086. International Joint Conferences on Artificial Intelligence Organization, Vienna, Austria (2022). https://www.ijcai.org/proceedings/2022/705. Accessed 1 May 2023
9. Jaynes, E.T.: Information theory and statistical mechanics. Phys. Rev. **106**(4), 620–630 (1957)
10. Lunardi, G.M., Machado, G.M., Maran, V., de Oliveira, J.P.M.: A metric for filter bubble measurement in recommender algorithms considering the news domain. Appl. Soft Comput. **97**, 106771 (2020)
11. Pariser, E.: The Filter Bubble: What the Internet is Hiding from You. Penguin UK, London, UK (2011)
12. Sindermann, C., Elhai, J.D., Moshagen, M., Montag, C.: Age, gender, personality, ideological attitudes and individual differences in a person's news spectrum: how many and who might be prone to "filter bubbles" and "echo chambers" online? Heliyon **6**(1), e03214 (2020)
13. Swearingen, K., Sinha, R.: Beyond algorithms: an HCI perspective on recommender systems. In: ACM SIGIR Workshop on Recommender Systems. New Orleans, Louisiana, USA (2001)
14. Vilela, A.L., Pereira, L.F.C., Dias, L., Stanley, H.E., Silva, L.R.D.: Majority-vote model with limited visibility: an investigation into filter bubbles. Phys. A Stat. Mech. Appl. **563**, 125450 (2021)
15. Wang, F., Zhu, H., Srivastava, G., Li, S., Khosravi, M.R., Qi, L.: Robust collaborative filtering recommendation with user-item-trust records. IEEE Trans. Comput.Soci. Syst. **9**(4), 986–996 (2021)
16. Zhao, X.: A study on e-commerce recommender system based on big data. In: 2019 IEEE 4th International Conference on Cloud Computing and Big Data Analysis. IEEE, Chengdu, China (2019). https://ieeexplore.ieee.org/document/8725694. Accessed 1 May 2023

Blockchain as a Collaborative Technology - Case Studies in the Real Estate Sector in Vietnam

Kha Nguyen Hoang[1], Trong Nguyen Duong Phu[1], Triet Nguyen Minh[1],
Huong Hoang Luong[1], Khoa Tran Dang[1], Khiem Huynh[1],
Phuc Nguyen Trong[1], Hieu Doan Minh[1], Quy Lu[1], Nguyen The Anh[1],
Ngan Nguyen Thi Kim[2], Hien Nguyen Quang[1], Bang Le Khanh[1],
Bao Tran Quoc[1], and Khanh Vo Hong[1(✉)]

[1] FPT University, Can Tho, Vietnam
khanhce171115@fpt.edu.vn, khanhvh@fe.edu.vn
[2] FPT Polytecnic, Can Tho, Vietnam

Abstract. This paper delves into the transformative potential of blockchain technology in the real estate sector, with a particular emphasis on Vietnam, a developing country with unique challenges. Traditional real estate processes in such contexts often suffer from issues such as lack of transparency, high intermediary fees, time-consuming document validation, and potential for fraud. These limitations create a pressing need for a more efficient, transparent, and secure system. In response to this, we explore the application of collaborative technologies, specifically blockchain and smart contracts, to redefine and streamline the real estate sector. We propose a novel model that leverages these technologies to address the identified issues. The model is designed to enhance transparency, reduce transaction times, and minimize the potential for fraud, thereby instilling greater trust in the real estate transaction process. This paper provides a comprehensive model for the real estate sector based on blockchain and smart contracts, addressing the specific challenges of the real estate sector in developing countries (i.e., Vietnam). We implement this model as a proof-of-concept on the Hyperledger Fabric platform, demonstrating its practical feasibility and benefits. Lastly, we evaluate the performance and efficiency of our model using the Hyperledger Caliper platform, providing valuable insights into its strengths and areas for potential improvement. The findings of this paper could significantly contribute to the evolution of the real estate sector in Vietnam and other similar markets, paving the social computing - in a case study of an efficient and secure real estate transaction process.

Keywords: Real estate · Blockchain · Smart contracts · Social computing · Hyperledger Fabric · Hyperledger Caliper

1 Introduction

The real estate sector plays a pivotal role in the economy of any country. For instance, in 2015, the real estate activities sector accounted for 1.9% of the total

S. Wu et al. (Eds.): PKAW 2023, LNAI 14317, pp. 111–123, 2023.
https://doi.org/10.1007/978-981-99-7855-7_9

workforce in the EU and 5.6% of the total number of enterprises [5]. This sector also significantly impacts social computing, influencing various societal aspects, including employment, housing, and urban development. However, traditional approaches to real estate have several limitations. For instance, Deedcoin, a blockchain-based service, aims to reduce the interaction fees between buyers and real estate agents from an average of 6% to a more attractive 1% [3]. Ubitquity, a Software-as-a-Service (SaaS) blockchain platform, aims to securely record asset information for clear notarization of ownership history [20]. Propy handles buyers and sellers for cross-border property transactions [1]. These services highlight the need for more efficient and secure real estate transactions [8].

Collaborative technologies, such as blockchain and smart contracts, can address these issues. Blockchain technology allows the transfer of tangible and intangible assets to a digital dimension, eliminating intermediaries and creating an economy where trust is not placed in a central authority or third party, but in complex cryptography [21]. Blockchain can enhance existing transaction processes, reduce the time required for negotiation and due diligence processes, and promote trust among stakeholders and reliability of information [22]. Smart contracts, which are self-executing and inherit security from the blockchain, can establish technical obligations and prevent parties from violating their obligations [16]. The use of blockchain technology in the real estate market has been gaining attention, with proposals for managing real estate through Color Coins, reusing the Bitcoin blockchain for other purposes [19].

Several countries have started applying blockchain and smart contracts to address traditional real estate problems. For instance, Sweden has launched a pilot project to evaluate potential blockchain applications for real estate transactions, which is predicted to save about 100 million euros [10,13,14]. The Netherlands has introduced several Blockchain pilots with real estate, including open data from cadastral and a government-wide pilot of the capabilities of the processes [10]. The Republic of Georgia was the first country to start registering land ownership using blockchain, with the aim of increasing the level of trust [10,17].

However, deploying blockchain-based real estate models in developing countries presents several challenges. For instance, Brazil lacks a modern integrated land registration system and faces challenges related to corruption and fraud [10]. Honduras announced a project in 2015 to use blockchain for land registration, but the project was never launched due to non-technological reasons [9,14]. These challenges need to be addressed to ensure the successful implementation of blockchain technology in the real estate sector.

This paper focuses on Vietnam as a case study. Despite the challenges, there is strong motivation for deploying a blockchain-based real estate system in Vietnam. The country has been making significant efforts to digitize its economy and stay competitive in the global market. The use of blockchain technology can eliminate many third-party factors that make real estate and cadastral work difficult [2].

The potential benefits of a blockchain-based real estate system in Vietnam are significant. It can improve the transparency and security of real estate transactions, reduce the fees associated with these transactions, and streamline the process of recording and transferring property ownership. This can lead to increased trust and confidence in the real estate sector, which in turn can stimulate economic growth and development. Therefore, we propose a blockchain-based model for the real estate sector in Vietnam, leveraging collaborative technology, i.e., blockchain and smart contracts. The main contributions of this paper are: (a) proposing a model of the Real Estate Sector based on Collaborative Technology in Vietnam; (b) implementing the proposed model (i.e., proof-of-concept) on the Hyperledger Fabric platform; and (c) evaluating the proposed model against the Hyperledger Caliper platform.

2   Related Work

2.1   Land Registration Systems Using Blockchain Technology

The first group primarily aims to utilize blockchain technology to enhance the transparency, efficiency, and trustworthiness of land and real estate registration systems.

Sweden's Lantmäteriet project. This project is a collaboration between Lantmäteriet (the Swedish Land Registry), ChromaWay (a blockchain technology company), Telia (a telecom company), and Kairos Future (a consultancy firm). Their goal is to streamline the process of real estate transactions by using blockchain technology. By focusing on the contractual process of a property sale, they hope to save time and reduce costs, ultimately leading to significant savings [10,13,14].

Republic of Georgia's Land Registration Project. In partnership with Bitfury Corporation (a blockchain technology provider), the National Public Registry (NAPR), and the Blockchain Trust Accelerator, Georgia became the first country to implement a blockchain-based land registration system. Their primary goal is to increase trust and transparency in land ownership and transactions. This project utilizes a Hybrid Blockchain system, where land registration data is initially recorded in a private Blockchain and then posted onto a public Blockchain [10,17].

Brazil's Cartório de Registro de Imóveis Project. This project is a partnership between the Brazilian real estate registry office and the blockchain technology company, Ubitquity. They aim to combat corruption and fraud in the land registration process by creating a parallel blockchain platform to mirror the existing legal asset recording and transfer processes [10].

While blockchain projects in land registration systems have shown promise in enhancing transparency and efficiency, they often face legal and institutional challenges. For example, the projects in Sweden, Georgia, and Brazil still rely heavily on existing governmental and legal structures. This reliance can limit the full potential of blockchain technology due to bureaucratic hurdles and legal constraints [14].

Our work contributes to this area by proposing a model specifically tailored for the real estate sector in Vietnam, based on collaborative technology. This approach aims to address the mentioned limitations by fostering increased involvement of various stakeholders, thereby reducing reliance on a single entity and paving the way for more decentralized and efficient operations. We then implement this model as a proof-of-concept on the Hyperledger Fabric platform, demonstrating its practical applicability [11,12].

2.2 Blockchain for Shared Ownership and Asset Management

This group includes projects that focus on using blockchain technology for shared property ownership and efficient asset management.

In the Netherlands, several blockchain pilots have been launched, focusing on providing open data from cadastral and government-wide pilot capabilities. Additionally, the Crowd Ownership Blandlord concept utilizes blockchain technology to enable shared property ownership in accordance with the principles of a sharing economy [10]. Moreover, REX is a U.S.-based firm that proposed a new diversified listing system (MLS) standard for real estate brokers using blockchain technology. This system aims to improve the transparency and efficiency of real estate transactions, making it easier for brokers to work together [9]. Projects focusing on shared property ownership and efficient asset management, such as those in the Netherlands and the REX initiative in the USA, are still in their nascent stages. They also face challenges related to regulatory compliance, scalability, and public acceptance [9].

Our contribution in this area lies in the implementation of our proposed model that not only addresses issues of shared property ownership but also efficiently manages these assets. The utilization of the Hyperledger Fabric platform, known for its scalability and security, allows our model to handle a significant volume of transactions and data, addressing some of the prevalent scalability issues [6,18].

2.3 Blockchain Initiatives for Comprehensive Asset Registration and Management

This topic groups projects that intend to use blockchain technology for the complete registration, management, and unification of assets.

Bitland's Initiative in Ghana. Bitland has started a project in Ghana with the intention of using blockchain technology to register land and real estate ownership. The ultimate goal is to eliminate intermediaries and create a global real estate supermarket powered by blockchain and smart contracts [9,13].

Japanese Government's Asset Unification Project. The Japanese government is exploring the use of blockchain technology to register and manage all data on properties, including vacant properties, inefficiently used land and spaces, and properties with unconfirmed tenants or users [17].

The initiatives for comprehensive asset registration and management, such as Bitland's in Ghana and the Japanese government's project, are ambitious but face issues related to cultural acceptance, comprehensive legal recognition, and technological infrastructure [13].

Our work aims to tackle these challenges by presenting a comprehensive model for asset registration and management that is adapted to the local cultural context of Vietnam. The proof-of-concept implementation on the Hyperledger Fabric platform demonstrates the technical feasibility of the proposed model. Further, we evaluate the proposed model against the Hyperledger Caliper platform to gauge its performance and scalability, thereby ensuring that it can handle the demands of a fully operational real estate sector [4,7,15].

3   Approach

In this section, we first summarize the traditional real estate management process applied in the developing countries (including Vietnam[1]) as well as propose a model based on blockchain technology and smart contracts to solve the limitations of the traditional model as well as NFT technology.

3.1   The Traditional Model of Real Estate

Figure 1 shows the traditional process of real estate management process including six components, namely Land Availability; Property Development; Real Estate Market; Government Regulations; Financing; and Infrastructure. The meaning of these components is presented below:

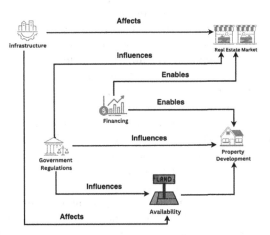

Fig. 1. Traditional real estate management diagram.

---

[1] We apply the most common model appy in the real estate company in Vietnam.

– **Land Availability (LA)**: This is the starting point of any real estate model. The availability of land for development is influenced by geographical factors, government regulations, and existing infrastructure.
– **Property Development (PD)**: Once land is available, property developers step in to build residential, commercial, or industrial properties. This process involves securing financing, planning and design, construction, and eventually sales or leasing.
– **Real Estate Market (REM)**: This is where properties are bought, sold, or rented. The market is influenced by supply and demand dynamics, which in turn are influenced by factors such as population growth, income levels, and economic conditions.
– **Government Regulations (GR)**: Governments in developing countries often play a significant role in the real estate market. They can influence the market through policies related to land use, building codes, taxation, and incentives for development.
– **Financing (F)**: Access to financing is a critical factor in the real estate market. This can come from banks, microfinance institutions, or other lenders. In many developing countries, access to credit can be a significant barrier to home ownership.
– **Infrastructure (I)**: The availability of infrastructure such as roads, utilities, and public services can greatly influence the value of real estate. In many developing countries, infrastructure development is a major challenge.

Let's go through the details of our summarized diagram. (**LA**) - This is the starting point of any real estate model. The availability of land for development is influenced by geographical factors, government regulations, and existing infrastructure. (**PD**) Once land is available, property developers step in to build residential, commercial, or industrial properties. This process involves securing financing, planning and design, construction, and eventually sales or leasing. (**REM**) - This is where properties are bought, sold, or rented. The market is influenced by supply and demand dynamics, which in turn are influenced by factors such as population growth, income levels, and economic conditions. (**GR**) - Governments in developing countries often play a significant role in the real estate market. They can influence the market through policies related to land use, building codes, taxation, and incentives for development. (**F**) - Access to financing is a critical factor in the real estate market. This can come from banks, microfinance institutions, or other lenders. In many developing countries, access to credit can be a significant barrier to home ownership. (**I**) - The availability of infrastructure such as roads, utilities, and public services can greatly influence the value of real estate. In many developing countries, infrastructure development is a major challenge. Each arrow in the diagram represents a relationship or influence between the components of the model, e.g., government regulations influence land availability, property development, and the real estate market.

Although, this diagram is applied in several cases but it still includes four main limitation:

- Lack of Transparency: In many developing countries (including Vietnam), the real estate sector suffers from a lack of transparency. This can lead to issues such as fraud, corruption, and disputes over property ownership.
- **Inefficient Processes**: The processes involved in buying, selling, or renting property can be slow and inefficient. This is often due to bureaucratic red tape and outdated systems.
- **Limited Access to Financing**: Many people in developing countries have limited access to credit, making it difficult for them to buy property.
- **Lack of Trust**: Due to the issues mentioned above, there can be a lack of trust in the real estate sector. This can discourage people from investing in property.

Based on these limitation, we proposed a Blockchain-based model that can potentially address these issues. Figure 2 shows a diagram for the real estate management model based on blockchain technology (i.e., Hyperledger Fabric) and smart contract (i.e., used Golang). The updated process is summarized in 5 components, including **Blockchain (Hyperledger Fabric) (BC)** - This is the underlying technology that supports the new model. It provides transparency, improves efficiency, facilitates financing, and enables social computing in the real estate market. **(REM)** - This is where properties are bought, sold, or rented. The market is influenced by the blockchain technology, which provides transparency and trust, improves efficiency, facilitates financing, and enables social computing. **(GR)** - Governments can influence the adoption and use of blockchain technology in the real estate market through policies and regulations. **(F)** - Access to financing is a critical factor in the real estate market. Blockchain technology can facilitate new forms of financing, such as peer-to-peer lending or fractional ownership of property. **Social Computing (SC)** - Blockchain technology can enable new forms of social computing in the real estate sector. For example, it can facilitate collaboration between different stakeholders, such as property developers, buyers, sellers, and government regulators.[2]

Our proposed model can be addressed the four limitation of the current traditional approach:

- **Transparency and Trust**: Blockchain technology can provide a transparent and immutable record of all transactions. This can help to build trust and prevent fraud.
- **Efficiency**: Blockchain can automate many of the processes involved in real estate transactions, making them faster and more efficient.
- **Access to Financing**: Blockchain can facilitate peer-to-peer lending or fractional ownership of property, potentially making it easier for people to access financing.

---

[2] Each arrow in the diagram represents a relationship or influence between the components of the model. For example, Hyperledger Fabric provides transparency and trust to the real estate market, and government regulations influence the adoption and use of blockchain technology.

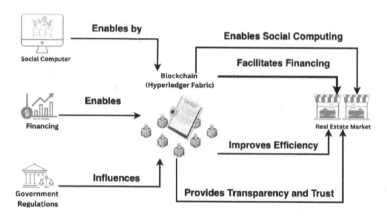

Fig. 2. Real estate management model based on blockchain technology and smart contract.

– **Social Computing**: Blockchain can enable new forms of social computing in the real estate sector. For example, it can facilitate collaboration between different stakeholders, such as property developers, buyers, sellers, and government regulators.

4   Evaluation

4.1   Environment Settings

Our model is deployed on Ubuntu 20.01 configuration, core i5 2.7Ghz, 8GB RAM. The proof-of-concept is implemented on the Hyperledger Fabric platform (HF) designed in docker containers. In this section, we measure the performance of chaincode in two scenarios, namely data initialization and querying.

To evaluate the performance of the proposed model, we also define some metrics by exploiting Hyperledger Caliper[3] Our measurements are based on five scenarios (from 1,000 requests per second to 5,000 requests per second). Specifically, we analyze the following parameters: Success and Fail requests, Send Rate - transaction per second (TPS); Max, Min, and Average Latency(s); and Throughput (TPS).

– Success and Fail: The number of successful and failed real estate transaction requests processed by the system. Successful transactions were accurately processed and stored in the blockchain, whereas failed transactions indicate transactions that could not be processed due to issues such as network problems or data inconsistencies.
– Send Rate (TPS): This represents the number of transactions per second that the system was able to handle, indicating the speed at which requests were processed.

---

[3] https://www.hyperledger.org/use/caliper.

– Max, Min, and Avg Latency (s): These metrics show the maximum, minimum, and average latency of transaction requests in seconds. Latency refers to the delay before a transfer of data begins following an instruction for its transfer. Lower latency implies faster transaction processing times.
– Throughput (TPS): The number of transactions processed per second, indicating the system's efficiency in handling transactions.

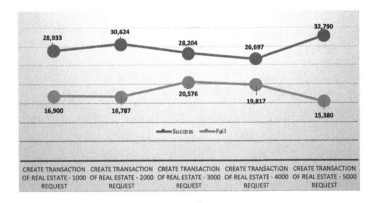

Fig. 3. Data creation of HF-based real estate model.

4.2   Data Creation

Figure 3 and Table 1 illustrate the performance metrics of our proposed HF-based real estate model, measured through five different scenarios of increasing load (from 1000 to 5000 requests). These requests represent the creation of real estate transactions in the system, and the subsequent metrics provide insights into the system's performance under varying loads.

In each of the scenarios, the system exhibited differing performance characteristics. For instance, in the scenario with 1000 requests, the system successfully processed 28,933 transactions, but failed to process 16,900. The send rate was 126.4 TPS, with the maximum, minimum, and average latency being 1,663.62 s, 0.49 s, and 648.60 s, respectively. The throughput was 19.5 TPS.

The highest send rate was achieved in the 3000 request scenario with 136.2 TPS. Interestingly, the scenario with the highest load (5000 requests) recorded the highest number of successful transactions (32,790) and the highest maximum latency (1,778.83 s), while maintaining a reasonable send rate and throughput.

These results provide valuable insights into the capabilities and limitations of our proposed HF-based real estate model, demonstrating its ability to process high volumes of transactions with acceptable latency and throughput levels while indicating potential areas for performance optimization.

Table 1. Data creation (i.e., transaction of real estate) of HF-based real estate model.

Name	Send Rate (TPS)	Max Latency (s)	Min Latency (s)	Avg Latency (s)	Throughput (TPS)
1000 request	126.4	1,663.62	0.49	648.60	19.5
2000 request	131.7	1,736.05	10.90	699.13	18.9
3000 request	136.2	1,598.66	11.91	630.59	22.8
4000 request	128.6	1,550.24	6.52	590.93	22.7
5000 request	134.2	1,778.83	6.13	705.88	19.1

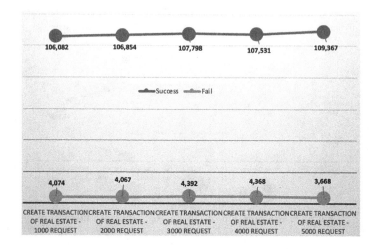

Fig. 4. Data query of HF-based real estate model.

4.3 Data Query

Figure 4 and Table 2 provide a detailed analysis of the performance metrics for data querying, i.e., the retrieval of real estate transactions, within our proposed HF-based real estate model. As with the previous table, these metrics were collected over five different scenarios, each with a different number of requests ranging from 1000 to 5000.

In each scenario, we observe distinct system performance characteristics. For instance, in the 1000 request scenario, 106,082 requests succeeded, and 4,074 requests failed. The send rate was 340.4 TPS, with a maximum latency of 420.36 s, minimum latency of 0.01 s, and an average latency of 4.92 s. The throughput was 290.20 TPS.

The 5000 request scenario handled the highest load with a send rate of 350.0 TPS, while it recorded the most significant number of successful transactions (109,367) and the highest throughput (299.90 TPS). The maximum, minimum, and average latencies remained consistent across all the scenarios.

Overall, these results provide crucial insights into the performance of our HF-based real estate model in managing data query transactions. The system demonstrates a robust capability to handle a high volume of data queries with a high success rate and a relatively low and stable latency, offering reliable real-time access to transaction data.

Table 2. Data query (i.e., transaction of real estate) of HF-based real estate model.

Name	Send Rate (TPS)	Max Latency (s)	Min Latency (s)	Avg Latency (s)	Throughput (TPS)
1000 requests	340.4	420.36	0.01	4.92	290.20
2000 requests	342.9	419.90	0.01	5.23	292.80
3000 requests	347.1	420.04	0.01	5.30	296.80
4000 requests	346.2	419.98	0.01	5.30	296.00
5000 requests	350.0	419.68	0.02	5.15	299.90

5 Conclusion

In conclusion, our study showcases the transformative potential of blockchain technology in the real estate industry, providing evidence for this emerging paradigm shift. By introducing a blockchain-based model for real estate management, we have presented a solid case for abandoning traditional systems in favor of smart contracts and decentralized networks. Our contribution to this field is threefold: i) we proposed a model that leverages blockchain and smart contracts to streamline real estate management processes in Vietnam, demonstrating an innovative alternative to conventional, centralized systems. The implementation of our model not only fosters transparency and security but also improves the overall efficiency of property transactions; ii) we have successfully implemented the proposed model as a proof-of-concept on the Hyperledger Fabric platform, one of the leading frameworks for developing blockchain applications. This serves to reinforce the practical viability of our model and highlights the adaptability of Hyperledger Fabric to diverse use cases; iii), we thoroughly evaluated the performance of our model using the Hyperledger Caliper benchmarking tool. The results revealed a stable success rate and acceptable latency levels under various loads, underscoring the model's scalability and robustness.

Our study ultimately highlights the compelling advantages of blockchain technology in real estate management, from improved transaction speed to enhanced security, thereby underscoring the transformative potential of this technology in the Vietnamese real estate sector. As we continue to refine our model and explore new use cases, we anticipate that our findings will foster further exploration and adoption of blockchain in real estate and other sectors. In closing, we hope that this research will pave the way for more in-depth studies and practical applications of blockchain technology, not only in real estate but across various industries, as we collectively move towards a more decentralized and collaborative future.

References

1. Propy - more secure. more efficient. more cost-effective. buy and sell real estate online secured through blockchain. https://propy.com
2. Averin, A., et al.: Review of existing solutions in the field of real estate and cadastral accounting based on blockchain technology. In: 2021 IT&QM&IS, pp. 144–147. IEEE (2021)

3. Deedcoin Team: Deedcoin white paper (2017). https://www.deedcoinlaunch.com/documents/Deedcoin_White_20Paper.pdf

4. Duong-Trung, N., et al.: Multi-sessions mechanism for decentralized cash on delivery system. Int. J. Adv. Comput. Sci. Appl. **10**(9), 553–560 (2019)

5. EUROSTAT: Real estate activity statistics - NACE Rev. 2 (2015). https://ec.europa.eu/eurostat/statistics-explained/index.php?title=Real_estate_activity_statistics_-_NACE_Rev._2&oldid=572702

6. Ha, X.S., Le, T.H., Phan, T.T., Nguyen, H.H.D., Vo, H.K., Duong-Trung, N.: Scrutinizing trust and transparency in cash on delivery systems. In: Wang, G., Chen, B., Li, W., Di Pietro, R., Yan, X., Han, H. (eds.) SpaCCS 2020. LNCS, vol. 12382, pp. 214–227. Springer, Cham (2021). https://doi.org/10.1007/978-3-030-68851-6_15

7. Ha, X.S., et al.: DeM-CoD: novel access-control-based cash on delivery mechanism for decentralized marketplace. In: the International Conference on Trust, Security and Privacy in Computing and Communications (TrustCom), pp. 71–78 (2020)

8. Karamitsos, I., et al.: Design of the blockchain smart contract: a use case for real estate. J. Inf. Secur. **9**(03), 177 (2018)

9. Konashevych, O.: Constraints and benefits of the blockchain use for real estate and property rights. J. Property Plann. Environ. Law **12**(2), 109–127 (2020)

10. Krupa, K.S.J., Akhil, M.S.: Reshaping the real estate industry using blockchain. In: Sridhar, V., Padma, M.C., Rao, K.A.R. (eds.) Emerging Research in Electronics, Computer Science and Technology. LNEE, vol. 545, pp. 255–263. Springer, Singapore (2019). https://doi.org/10.1007/978-981-13-5802-9_24

11. Le, H.T., et al.: Introducing multi shippers mechanism for decentralized cash on delivery system. Int. J. Adv. Comput. Sci. Appl. **10**(6), 590–597 (2019)

12. Le, N.T.T., et al.: Assuring non-fraudulent transactions in cash on delivery by introducing double smart contracts. Int. J. Adv. Comput. Sci. Appl. **10**(5), 677–684 (2019)

13. Mezquita, Y., Parra, J., Perez, E., Prieto, J., Corchado, J.M.: Blockchain-based systems in land registry, a survey of their use and economic implications. In: Herrero, Á., Cambra, C., Urda, D., Sedano, J., Quintián, H., Corchado, E. (eds.) CISIS 2019. AISC, vol. 1267, pp. 13–22. Springer, Cham (2021). https://doi.org/10.1007/978-3-030-57805-3_2

14. Nasarre-Aznar, S.: Collaborative housing and blockchain. Administration **66**(2), 59–82 (2018)

15. Quynh, N.T.T., et al.: Toward a design of blood donation management by blockchain technologies. In: Gervasi, O., et al. (eds.) ICCSA 2021. LNCS, vol. 12956, pp. 78–90. Springer, Cham (2021). https://doi.org/10.1007/978-3-030-87010-2_6

16. Savelyev, A.: Contract law 2.0: 'Smart' contracts as the beginning of the end of classic contract law. Inf. Commun. Technol. Law **26**(2), 116–134 (2017)

17. Shang, Q., Price, A.: A blockchain-based land titling project in the republic of Georgia: Rebuilding public trust and lessons for future pilot projects. Innovations Technol. Gov. Globalization **12**(3–4), 72–78 (2019)

18. Son, H.X., Le, T.H., Quynh, N.T.T., Huy, H.N.D., Duong-Trung, N., Luong, H.H.: Toward a blockchain-based technology in dealing with emergencies in patient-centered healthcare systems. In: Bouzefrane, S., Laurent, M., Boumerdassi, S., Renault, E. (eds.) MSPN 2020. LNCS, vol. 12605, pp. 44–56. Springer, Cham (2021). https://doi.org/10.1007/978-3-030-67550-9_4

19. Spielman, A.: Blockchain: Digitally Rebuilding the Real Estate Industry. Ph.D. thesis, Massachusetts Institute of Technology (2016)

20. Ubitquity: Ubitquity® the enterprise-ready blockchain-secured platform for real estate recordkeeping https://www.ubitquity.io
21. Veuger, J.: Trust in a viable real estate economy with disruption and blockchain. Facilities **36**(1) (2018)
22. Wouda, H.P., Opdenakker, R.: Blockchain technology in commercial real estate transactions. J. Property Investment Finance **37**(6), 570–579 (2019)

Indonesian Forest Fire Data Clustering Using Spatiotemporal Data Using Grid Density-Based Clustering Algorithm

Devi Fitrianah[1], Hisyam Fahmi[2], Ade Putera Kemala[1（✉）],
and Muhammad Edo Syahputra[1]

[1] Bina Nusantara University, Jakarta 14480, Indonesia
`ade.kemala@binus.ac.id`
[2] UIN Maulana Malik Ibrahim University, Malang 65144, Indonesia

Abstract. Forest fires are major environmental issues, especially in Indonesia which has the large area of forests. It becomes national problems that must be integrally and systematically resolved. Forest fires prediction and mapping are one of the approaches providing information about potential forest fire areas. The meteorological conditions (e.g., temperature, wind speed, humidity) are known features influencing forest fires to spread. In this research, we combine the information from meteorological data and the forest fires incident in Indonesia for a specific location and time to map and predict forest fire areas. Forest fires data obtained from BNPB website from 2011 until 2023 and then combined with meteorological data at the corresponding time. Grouping closest points into one cluster is the first step to map the data using IMSTAGRID algorithm. This algorithm is the adaptation of the grid density clustering method implemented for spatiotemporal data which provides a good clustering result with Silhouette values up to 0.8175.

Keywords: Forest Fires · Spatiotemporal · Data Mining · Grid Density Based Clustering · HDBSCAN

1 Introduction

Indonesia is a country with a large area of forest and a tropical climate, which often causes forest fires every year. Forest fires have numerous consequences, many of which are detrimental to humans and other ecosystems. Forest fires can affect ecological, climate change, economic and health effects [1]. Fires can destroy the habitat of animals, especially endangered wildlife in Indonesia. The ozone problem in the troposphere is influenced by smoke from fires as well, which can affect climate change. Fire smog causes considerable economic losses, such as tourism, agriculture, forestry, health, and the transport sector, because of poor visibility and heavy breathing [1]. According to the Indonesian National Board for Disaster Management, as of February of 2023 alone there has been 30 occurrences of forest fire in Indonesia. While the most severe year of forest fires in Indonesia happened in 2019 with 757 occurrences.

© The Author(s), under exclusive license to Springer Nature Singapore Pte Ltd. 2023
S. Wu et al. (Eds.): PKAW 2023, LNAI 14317, pp. 124–133, 2023.
https://doi.org/10.1007/978-981-99-7855-7_10

Forest fires can be caused by natural causes or intentionally by humans. Human-caused forest fires should be prevented and punished by the legal system, but environmental causes can be predicted and avoided. Climate is one of many natural factors that can cause forest fires because it influences the level of surface fuel dryness, the amount of oxygen, and the rate at which the fire spreads [2]. As a result, an effort should be made to overcome this disaster; one approach is to develop an early warning system using spatiotemporal projection and predict the characteristics of potential forest fire areas (Fig. 1).

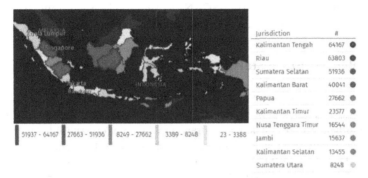

Jurisdiction	#	
Kalimantan Tengah	64167	●
Riau	63803	●
Sumatera Selatan	51936	●
Kalimantan Barat	40041	●
Papua	27662	●
Kalimantan Timur	23577	●
Nusa Tenggara Timur	16544	◐
Jambi	15637	●
Kalimantan Selatan	13455	●
Sumatera Utara	8248	◌

| 51937 - 64167 | 27663 - 51936 | 8249 - 27662 | 3389 - 8248 | 23 - 3388 |

Fig. 1. Greatest Number of Fire Alerts by Province (Jan 2013–July 2018) (Global Forest Watch 2014)

The spatiotemporal projection is generated by mapping the values of a 3-dimensional and time-evolving physical quantity into a 2-dimensional space with spatial and temporal axes [3]. Spatiotemporal data mining is broadly used to reveal patterns or phenomena of natural events such as the identification of earthquake disaster areas, forest fires identification, and mapping of potential fishing zones [4]. The clustered results of spatiotemporal mapping will be combined with meteorological features for the corresponding location to predict potential forest fire areas. The meteorological features that are used, for example, temperature, wind, humidity.

Therefore, in this research, we begin by analyzing the causes of forest fires and then develop a system to perform clustering on the dataset using the Imstagrid algorithm [5]. The system utilizes spatiotemporal clustering to cluster the forest fire locations. Meteorological features are combined with the clustering results to create a model that can cluster data and, hopefully, predict the potential area of forest fire in the future.

2 Previous Study

The study of forest fires has been widely implemented by many researchers around the world, which mostly utilize sensory technology. Umamaheshwaran proposed an image mining method using images from the Meteosat-SEVIRI sensor that produced a linear model of forest fires with vegetation and wind direction [6].

A study of the parameters influencing the forest fire process is also being conducted in order to formulate the characteristics of forest fire types. Time of fire, land cover type, altitude of forest land, slope of land, and forest fire statistics are all factors that can influence forest fires. This model has been validated using data from NOAA-AVHRR and Terra MODIS satellites [7]. Another point that needs to be considered in determining potential forest fire is the size of the grid from the image used against existing weather observations [8]. Another study of forest fire-related variables is how to determine the linkages between land cover types and vegetation with fires [9]. The study succeeded in describing the potential vegetation types of forest fires by using imagery from satellite sensing.

Huang et al. conducted research in high-risk areas to understand the spatial distribution of high fire risk using the HDBSCAN algorithm and early warning weather [10]. The data came from satellite data of Yunnan Province during 2015–2019.

3   Spatiotemporal Clustering

Spatiotemporal clustering is one method for analyzing spatiotemporal data. Clustering spatiotemporal data can be done directly in 3-dimensional space (time and 2-dimensional space) or alternatively, i.e., in new temporal-spatial data or otherwise [11].

The most widely used spatiotemporal clustering method for analyzing large spatiotemporal datasets is DBSCAN. It has the ability to find clusters of varying shapes such as linear, oval, concave and other shapes. DBSCAN, unlike other clustering algorithms, does not require the number of clusters to be determined. Birant and Kut proposed S-DBSCAN that improves the performance of DBSCAN by adding 3 marginal extras in DBSCAN to identify core objects, noise objects and adjacent clusters [12].

The spatiotemporal clustering method used for the data of natural phenomena and adjusting to the nature of the data is one of the methods developed based on density and grid. This method proved very robust to handle data of different data types with the result of accuracy reach 82.68% [4].

4   Data, Method, and Implementation of Imstagrid

4.1   Data

The forest fire data utilized in this study is spatiotemporal data which is combined with meteorological data at Indonesian area taken from August 2011 to 2023. The forest fire data obtained from BNPB website [16] includes longitude, latitude, date, month, and year.

Using the obtained latitude and longitude data, meteorological features of the location can be obtained from World Weather Online websites. The site provides a REST API for accessing weather data since July 1, 2008. The API is accessed under the "GET" method and will return weather components such as air temperature (in Celsius and Fahrenheit), weather description, weather icon, and wind speed in JSON (JavaScript Object Notation) format, XML, or CSV. Intake of weather data can be taken by city name, IP address, latitude, and longitude coordinates (in decimal), for UK, US, and Canadian countries can use zip code (World Weather Online 2008).

List parameters of the final dataset comprise of 14 features which are Year, Month, Day, Latitude, Longitude, tempC (temperature), precipMM (precipitation), humidity, cloudcover, HeatIndexC, DewPointC, windspeedKmph, WindGustKmph and aggregate Time with a total of 2846 rows of data. Despite the extensive range of features encompassed by this dataset, it is not without shortcomings. One notable limitation pertains to the unknown extent of severity in the forest fire data, which creates uncertainty regarding the potential impact of the fires on weather conditions. The influence of these fires on weather patterns remains unknown. It is conceivable to treat this type of data as an anomaly or outlier; however, given the dataset size, it is unlikely to exert a substantial influence on the overall results. Figure 2 shows the plot of the forest fire dataset used in this research.

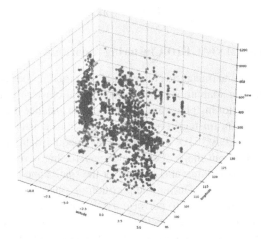

Fig. 2. Dataset Visualization

4.2 Method

In this study we take several steps to get to the results. Our study consists of 5 phases as illustrated in Fig. 3. For the data acquisition step we collect the data from BNPB website which is a government instantion for disaster management. Then, the dataset is cleaned and the resulting data is used to train IMSTAGRID. The created cluster is analysed for the best parameters combination and validated using silhouette index method.

4.3 HDBSCAN

HDBSCAN (Hierarchical Density-Based Spatial Clustering of Applications with Noise) [13] is a developed version of DBSCAN [14] algorithm which is used for clustering purposes. HDBSCAN improves density-based clustering method by establishing a hierarchical representation of the clusters [15], the algorithm's execution produces a hierarchy that can be effectively utilized for cluster extraction and outlier detection. HDBSCAN

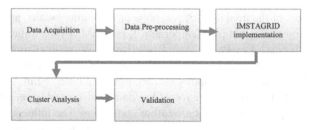

Fig. 3. Methodology

addresses the limitations of DBSCAN by enabling the identification of clusters with varying densities. For this research, we will use HDBSCAN algorithm as the baseline to compare how well the Imstagrid algorithm works.

4.4   Implementation IMSTAGRID Clustering Algorithm

In this study, we adopted the Imstagrid clustering algorithm for processing the spatiotemporal forest fire data. The adaptations for spatiotemporal clustering from the Imstagrid algorithm are in the partitioning phase and computing the distance threshold (r). In terms of partitioning mechanism, Imstagrid outperforms previous clustering methods such as ST-AGRID [4]. Using ST-AGRID would result in unequal data spread and interval, resulting in cells in a different shape of cube and gaps. Imstagrid overcame this problem by recommending a uniform interval (L) value for the spatial and temporal dimensions, resulting in a cube-shaped cell. During the partitioning phase, the data space/object is divided into cubes. It is necessary to perform a cubes interval calculation when determining the number of cubes. The cubes interval (L) value is obtained by dividing each dimension range (upper bound - lower bound) by the number of m cells. The number of intervals (L) is only for spatial dimensions (longitude and latitude), whereas for temporal dimensions, the cell interval for the dimension is using aggregate temporal due to its data structure. Unlike the AGRID+ [5] algorithm approach, which uses only one distance threshold value, the Imstagrid algorithm suggests a unique distance threshold for each dimension (spatial and temporal). Finally, Imstagrid improves the density compensation calculation, which determines the density threshold to determine whether or not a group is a cluster.

As each cube (spatial and temporal) is formed, each data object is stored in each cube that is relevant to its spatiotemporal coordinates. The phase is then adjusted in order to compute the distance threshold (r). Computing the distance threshold much depends on the partitioning phase in finding the value of L.

Where λ is interval weight parameter used, L is interval, and ϵ is a small integer number, so that the value of $r < L/2$. After the adaptation step has been done, the rest of the steps will be implemented similarly to those in the AGRID+.

In this step of our study, our clustering algorithm, IMSTAGRID is an improvement of the ST-AGRID applied to the forest fire dataset.

(1) **Partitioning.** The entire data space of forest fire data, which includes the location and time of fire, is partitioned into cells based on m which is the number of cells and p. The coordinates of each object are then assigned to a cube, and non-empty cubes are inserted into a hash table. The cube is a data structure with three dimensions (spatial and temporal), the first two of which are longitude and latitude, and the third of which is time.

(2) **Computing distance threshold.** Determine the neighbourhood radius (r) for each data point to other data point in a neighbour. After that we have and based on the appropriate time unit.

(3) **Calculating densities.** For each object of data, count the number of objects both in its neighboring cells and in its neighbourhood as its density.

(4) **Compensating Densities.** For each object of data compute the ratio of the volume of all neighbours and that of neighbours considered and use the product of the ratio and the density of the cell as the new density.

(5) **Calculating density threshold (DT).** The average of all compensated densities is calculated and then the DT is computed by finding the average of the density compensation divided by theta parameters which are coefficients that can be tuned in to get a different cluster level.

(6) **Clustering automatically.** First, each object with a density greater than DT is considered a cluster. Then, for each object, examine each object in the neighboring cells to see if its density exceeds the density threshold and its distance from the object exceeds the distance threshold. If yes, then merge the two clusters to which the two objects belong. Continue the merging procedure described above until all eligible object pairs have been checked.

4.5 Hyperparameter Search

Both the HDBSCAN and Imstagrid algorithms use different hyperparameters that can be tuned to improve clustering results. In this step, we use the Gridsearch method to try and find the best parameters for each algorithm. Tables 1. and 2. show the hyperparameter search space for HDBSCAN and Imstagrid, respectively.

Table 1. HDBSCAN hyperparameters search

Hyperparameter	Search Space
Min_samples	[2, 3, 4, 5, 6, 7, 8, 9]
Min_cluster_size	[2, 3, 4, 5, 6, 7, 8, 9, 10, 12]
Cluster_selection_epsilon	[0.1, 0.2, 0.3, 0.4, 0.5, 0.8, 0.9]
Cluster_selection_method	['eom', 'leaf']

Table 2. Imstagrid hyperparameter search

Hyperparameter	Search Space
L_spasial	[6, 7, 8, 9, 10, 11, 12, 13, 14, 15, 16, 17, 18, 19, 20, 21, 22, 23, 24, 25]
Theta	[100, 90, 80, 60, 50, 40, 35, 30, 15, 5]
Lambda	[0.2, 0.5, 0.7, 0.8, 0.9]

4.6 Evaluation

The method that will be used to evaluate the clustering model is called silhouette analysis. This method calculates the silhouette index by using the density level within a cluster (intra-cluster distance) and the distance between each cluster (inter-cluster distance).

The best achievable value for the silhouette index is 1, while the lowest value is −1. If the silhouette score approaches 0, it indicates a significant overlap between clusters. Formula 1 shows the way to calculate the silhouette index.

$$Si \frac{bi - ai}{\max(bi, ai)} \tag{1}$$

Si = The silhouette score for data point i
bi = The inter-cluster distance for data point i
ai = The intra-cluster distance for data point i.

5 Results

For the HDBSCAN baseline method, a grid search was performed to determine the optimal hyperparameters. The results yielded the following values: min_samples: 9, min_cluster_size: 3, cluster_selection_epsilon: 0.1, and cluster_selection_method: 'leaf'. The silhouette score obtained for this configuration is 0.5965, it can be understood that HDBSCAN struggled to perform clustering task on this dataset. Figure 4 illustrates the visualization of the clustering outcome.

Table 3. shows the best hyperparameters obtained using the Gridsearch method for the Imstagrid algorithm. 100 different combinations of hyperparameters were investigated and the six best scenarios were displayed on Table 3.. This method yielded the highest silhouette score of 0.8175, which outperformed our baseline model. Furthermore, significant observations can be drawn from the data presented in Table 3.. The clustering results improve as the values of L, lambda, and theta increase. It is worth noting, however, that the theta value has a limit of 30 above which the silhouette score does not improve further. Figure 5 depicts the clustering results obtained using the Imstagrid algorithm.

Table 3. Imstagrid Hyperparameter Search Result

Scenario	L	Agg	Lambda	Theta	Silhouette Score
1	24	1	0.9	30	0.8124
2	24	1	0.9	60	0.8124
3	24	1	0.9	100	0.8124
4	25	1	0.9	30	0.8175
5	25	1	0.9	60	0.8175
6	25	1	0.9	100	0.8175

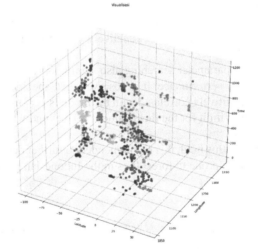

Fig. 4. HDBSCAN Clustering result

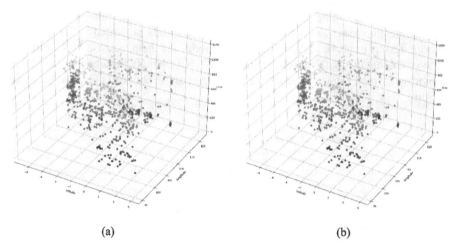

(a)   (b)

Fig. 5. a) Scenario 1 Visualization b) Scenario 3 Visualization

6   Conclusion

Real-world data gathering in research demonstrates that conventional algorithms, such as HDBSCAN, may not necessarily perform well in analyzing datasets. This research has successfully obtained information indicating that the Imstagrid method exhibits adequate performance and capability in effectively analyzing and clustering datasets with silhouette score of 0.8175.

The process of hyperparameter searching also significantly influences the improvement of the final model's performance. It is observed that, specifically for this dataset, higher values of L are positively correlated with the model's performance. Furthermore, it is known that the upper limit for the theta value is 30, beyond which the performance does not further improve.

For future research in this field, it is recommended to further develop the analysis of data and mapping of areas prone to forest fires in the Indonesian region.

References

1. Hirschberger, P.: Forests ablaze: causes and effects of global forest fires. WWF: Berlin, Germany (2016)
2. Syaufina, L., Hafni, D.A.F.: Variability of climate and forest and peat fires occurrences in Bengkalis Regency, Riau. J. Trop. Silviculture **9**(1), 60–68 (2018). VARIABILITAS IKLIM DAN KEJADIAN KEBAKARAN HUTAN DAN LAHAN GAMBUT DI KABUPATEN BENGKALIS, PROVINSI RIAU
3. Nakamura Miyamura, H., Hayashi, S., Suzuki, Y., Takemiya, H.: Spatio-temporal mapping - a technique for overview visualization of time-series datasets. Progress Nuclear Sci. Technol. **2**, 603–608 (2011)
4. Fitrianah, D., Hidayanto, A.N., Fahmi, H., Lumban Gaol, J., Arymurthy, A.M.: ST-AGRID: a spatio temporal grid density based clustering and its application for determining the potential fishing zones. Int. J. Softw. Eng. Appl. **9**(1), 13–26 (2015). https://doi.org/10.14257/ijseia. 2015.9.1.02

5. Fitrianah, D., Fahmi, H., Hidayanto, A.N., Arymurthy, A.M.: Improved partitioning technique for density cube-based spatio-temporal clustering method. J. King Saud Univ. Comput. Inf. Sci. **34**(10), 8234–8244 (2022). https://doi.org/10.1016/j.jksuci.2022.08.006

6. Umamaheshwaran, R., Bijker, W., Stein, A.: Image mining for modeling of forest fires from Meteosat images. IEEE Trans. Geosci. Remote Sens. **45**(1), 246–253 (2007). https://doi.org/10.1109/TGRS.2006.883460

7. Hernández-Leal, P.A., González-Calvo, A., Arbelo, M., Barreto, A., Alonso-Benito, A.: Synergy of GIS and remote sensing data in forest fire danger modeling. IEEE J. Sel. Top Appl. Earth Obs. Remote Sens. **1**(4), 240–247 (2008). https://doi.org/10.1109/JSTARS.2008.200 9043

8. Khabarov, N., Moltchanova, E., Obersteiner, M.: Valuing weather observation systems for forest fire management. IEEE Syst. J. **2**(3), 349–357 (2008). https://doi.org/10.1109/JSYST. 2008.925979

9. Tanase, M.A., Gitas, I.Z.: An examination of the effects of spatial resolution and image analysis technique on indirect fuel mapping. IEEE J. Sel. Top Appl. Earth Obs. Remote Sens. **1**(4), 220–229 (2008). https://doi.org/10.1109/JSTARS.2009.2012475

10. Huang, J., et al.: Fire risk assessment and warning based on hierarchical density-based spatial clustering algorithm and grey relational analysis. Math. Probl. Eng. **2022** (2022). https://doi. org/10.1155/2022/7339312

11. Abraham, T., Roddick, J.: Opportunities for knowledge discovery in spatio-temporal information systems. Australas. J. Inf. Syst. **5**(2), (1998). https://doi.org/10.3127/ajis.v5i2.338

12. Birant, D., Kut, A.: ST-DBSCAN: an algorithm for clustering spatial-temporal data. Data Knowl. Eng. **60**(1), 208–221 (2007). https://doi.org/10.1016/j.datak.2006.01.013

13. Campello, R.J.G.B., Moulavi, D., Zimek, A., Sander, J.: Hierarchical density estimates for data clustering, visualization, and outlier detection. ACM Trans. Knowl. Discov. Data **10**(1), 1–51 (2015). https://doi.org/10.1145/2733381

14. Daszykowski, M., Walczak, B.: A density-based algorithm for discovering cluster in large spatial databases with noise. In: Comprehensive Chemometrics: Chemical and Biochemical Data Analysis, Second Edition: Four Volume Set, vol. 2, pp. 565–580 (1996). https://doi.org/ 10.1016/B978-0-444-64165-6.03005-6

15. Stewart, G., Al-Khassaweneh, M.: An implementation of the HDBSCAN* clustering algorithm. Appl. Sci. (Switzerland) **12**(5), 1–21 (2022). https://doi.org/10.3390/app12052405

16. BNPB. Data bencana Indonesia [Internet]. [cited 2023 May 15]. Available from: https://dibi. bnpb.go.id/xdibi

Balanced Graph Structure Information for Brain Disease Detection

Falih Gozi Febrinanto[1]([✉]) [ID], Mujie Liu[1] [ID], and Feng Xia[2] [ID]

[1] Institute of Innovation, Science, and Sustainability,
Federation University Australia, Ballarat, Australia
{f.febrinanto,mujie.liu}@federation.edu.au
[2] School of Computing Technologies, RMIT University, Melbourne, Australia
f.xia@ieee.org

Abstract. Analyzing connections between brain regions of interest (ROI) is vital to detect neurological disorders such as autism or schizophrenia. Recent advancements employ graph neural networks (GNNs) to utilize graph structures in brains, improving detection performances. Current methods use correlation measures between ROI's blood-oxygen-level-dependent (BOLD) signals to generate the graph structure. Other methods use the training samples to learn the optimal graph structure through end-to-end learning. However, implementing those methods independently leads to some issues with noisy data for the correlation graphs and overfitting problems for the optimal graph. In this work, we proposed **Bargrain** (balanced graph structure for brains), which models two graph structures: filtered correlation matrix and optimal sample graph using graph convolution networks (GCNs). This approach aims to get advantages from both graphs and address the limitations of only relying on a single type of structure. Based on our extensive experiment, Bargrain outperforms state-of-the-art methods in classification tasks on brain disease datasets, as measured by average F1 scores.

Keywords: Brain Network · Classification · Graph Learning · Graph Neural Networks · Disease Detection

1 Introduction

Resting-state functional magnetic resonance imaging (Rest fMRI) analysis is vital for detecting brain diseases such as autism or schizophrenia in individuals [2, 10,11]. FMRI data measures changes in blood oxygen level-dependent signals (BOLD) over a specific time, providing essential information on brain activity [5, 8]. These BOLD signals represent variations in blood oxygen levels in different regions of interest (ROI), which are generated using several atlas techniques to divide the brain into distinct regions [5,14]. Researchers have a huge consensus on analyzing interactions between regions in brain networks as a key to a better diagnosis for detecting brain diseases.

Graph neural networks (GNN) have shown promising results in improving performance to predict diseases in the brain networks [3,11]. However, there is

© The Author(s), under exclusive license to Springer Nature Singapore Pte Ltd. 2023
S. Wu et al. (Eds.): PKAW 2023, LNAI 14317, pp. 134–143, 2023.
https://doi.org/10.1007/978-981-99-7855-7_11

still a challenge in defining the appropriate structure of graphs in brain networks. Some methods [5,14] adopt a correlation matrix to generate graphs that calculate the similarity between series of BOLD signals across all brain regions. This technique has a good aspect in incorporating biological insight or actual domain knowledge of brain structure. However, this technique potentially leads to inaccurate correlations matrix due to some noise caused by scanner drift or physiological noise that arises from cardiac pulsation, shifts caused by the body's motion [8]. Other methods [10,11,13] disregard the domain knowledge structure and instead utilize a learnable graph structure to search for optimal structures over variations in sample data through an end-to-end learning process, making it resistant to noise. However, these methods fail to enhance the interpretability of biological insights into graph structures and lack generalization to unseen data samples, making them prone to overfitting to training samples [1].

To address those problems, we propose a framework that utilizes balanced structure graphs for brain disease classification, called **Bargrain** (balanced graph structure for brains)[1]. It combines predefined signal correlation and learnable methods to generate the graph, aiming for both brain network information advantages. Our model applies a *filtered correlation matrix graph* based on signal similarities and an *optimal sampling graph* based on the Gumbel reparameterization trick [9]. This helps us prevent the noise issues in solely using domain knowledge structure and overfitting problems from just relying on learning optimal structure. We leverage effective node features derived from the ROIs' correlation matrix and employ graph convolutional networks (GCN) [17] for modeling the graph structures. We also use a graph readout function based on a CONCAT pooling operator since the disease prediction is a graph-level task. We summarize the main contribution of this paper as follows:

- We propose Bargain, a brain disease detection framework that utilizes a balanced graph structure by merging two valuable insights: actual domain knowledge structure and optimal structure of brain networks.
- We conduct an extensive experiment on real-world brain datasets. Our experimental results demonstrate that our method outperforms state-of-the-art models in classifying brain diseases.
- We systematically review how the two graph structures differ in network visualizations and node degree distributions, which enhances brain disease detection by using their complementary information.

2   Related Work

2.1   GNNs for Brain Disease Detection

Graph Neural Networks (GNNs) have demonstrated impressive performance in tackling various detection tasks involving graph data, including their application in healthcare for detecting brain diseases [15]. To represent the graph structure

---

[1] The implementation of Bargrain: https://github.com/falihgoz/Bargrain.

in the brain, the correlation matrix is a common method used to define the connectivity between ROIs. For example, GDC-GCN [5] follows the correlation calculation to create a graph structure and uses a graph diffusion technique to reduce noisy structures. BrainGNN [14] develops ROI-aware GNNs to utilize a special pooling strategy to select important nodes. On the other hand, instead of using predefined graphs, FBNetGen [10] explores a learnable graph to create brain networks and investigate some downstream tasks. Besides, DGM [13] designs a latent-graph learning block to build a probabilistic graph. Inspired by the advantages of graph transformers, BrainNETTF [11] capitalizes on the distinctive characteristics of brain network data.

2.2   Learnable Graph Generations

Learnable graph generation strategy aims to create optimal graphs through an end-to-end learning process. In practical scenarios, the graph structure is not always available or might be incomplete [6,16]. On top of that, even if a predefined graph structure exists, it might not provide the necessary information or align with the requirements of downstream tasks. Precisely, a learnable graph generation adjusts its structure based on the available data of all nodes, capturing intricate relationships that predefined graphs could overlook [1]. This adaptability improves the model's capability to unveil subtle, data-specific connections from provided samples, which can help mitigate noise in the predefined graph structure.

   Some techniques use a learnable node representation to calculate cosine similarity between those representations and optimize them during the learning process [10,13]. However, most of them apply the top-k closest relations to maintain graph sparsity, which impedes the designs of model flexibility and potentially eliminates some vital information. Therefore, considering the inequality of the information problem [18] in the message-passing process, the optimal sampling techniques [16] based on categorical reparameterization trick [9], which enables the approximation of samples from a categorical distribution, is introduced as an alternative to improve the flexibility by not selecting the top-k nearest nodes.

2.3   Framework Overview

Bargrain's overall framework is shown in Fig. 1. Based on our proposed method, there are 3 modules to classify brain disease.

- **Brain Signal Preprocessing**. We calculate the correlation matrix among the brain's regions of interest (ROIs). The developed correlation matrix will serve as both node features and the foundation for generating graph structure in the subsequent phase.
- **Graph Modeling**. Our objective is to balance the information employing both graph structures. We perform two graph structure generations: filtered correlation matrix graph and optimal sampling graph. The next step is to

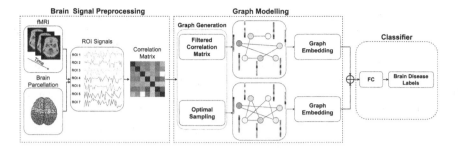

Fig. 1. The proposed framework. *Bargrain* starts with *Brain Signal Preprocessing* to develop a correlation matrix based on ROI signals. *Graph Modeling* processes two graph structures to balance information from domain knowledge and optimal structures. *Classifier* maps the combined knowledge for brain disease detection.

learn the spatial information for each graph structure using a graph convolution network (GCN). The resulting two graph-level representations, after the pooling process, will be used in the next module.

- **Classifier.** This step aims to combine two graph-level representations and map the combined knowledge to perform brain disease classification.

3   Proposed Framework

3.1   Brain Signal Preprocessing

Each brain's ROI produces signal series, and overall signals are represented by matrix $X \in \mathbb{R}^{N \times T}$, where N is the number of nodes (ROIs), and T represents a period of recording time. From these signal series, a correlation matrix $V \in \mathbb{R}^{N \times N}$ is generated to assess the similarity signals between ROIs. Moreover, the correlation values are utilized as node features in the graph, demonstrating a significant performance in detecting brain diseases [5,11].

3.2   Graph Modeling

Graph Generation. To balance the information about the graph structure, our framework's graph generation process is divided into two: *filtered correlation matrix graph* and *optimal sampling graph*.

The *filtered correlation matrix graph* aims to preserve the actual domain knowledge of the brain structure. The adjacency matrix of this graph type denotes as $A^{\text{filtered}} \in \mathbb{R}^{N \times N}$. To maintain the sparsity of the graph, it is obtained by comparing the correlation matrix $V \in \mathbb{R}^{N \times N}$ with a specific threshold c, as follows:

$$A_{ij}^{\text{filtered}} = \begin{cases} 1 & \text{if } V_{ij} > c; \\ 0 & \text{otherwise} \end{cases} \tag{1}$$

The *optimal sampling graph* aims to find the optimal structure based on the given training samples of the brain ROIs through an end-to-end learning process. The adjacency matrix of this type of graph is denoted as $A^{\text{optimal}} \in \mathbb{R}^{N \times N}$. The binary values in adjacency matrix $A \in \{0,1\}^{N \times N}$ are originally non-differentiable with the typical backpropagation due to their discrete nature. To solve this problem, the Gumbel reparameterization trick [9] was proposed. With that idea, we employ the Gumbel reparameterization trick to sample the optimal graph structure in the brain network. The Gumbel reparameterization trick to learn the graph structure is as follows:

$$A_{ij}^{\text{optimal}} = \text{sigmoid}((log(\theta_{ij}/(1 - \theta_{ij})) + (g_{ij}^1 - g_{ij}^2)/\tau), \qquad (2)$$

where θ_{ij} is learnable features vector based on node v_i and v_j, $g_{ij}^1, g_{ij}^2 \sim$ Gumbel(0,1) for all i,j, and τ represents temperature to control Gumbel distribution. High sigmoid probability represents a relation $A_{ij}^{\text{optimal}} = 1$ or 0 otherwise. As mentioned above, θ_{ij} is a learnable feature vector based on two nodes v_i and v_j. We perform a feature extraction mechanism [16] to encode signal representation in each ROI node v_i to a vector h_i for each i. We concatenate two embedding node vectors and apply two fully connected layers so that $\theta_{ij} = FC(FC(h^i || h^j))$.

Calculating the similarity between the brain's ROIs in the filtered correlation matrix graph generation will result in an undirected graph structure. It differs from the optimal sampling graph that results in a directed graph structure due to its sampling process.

Graph Embedding. We utilize a 2-layer graph convolutional networks (GCN) [17] to model the spatial information in the generated brain networks. The reason for using the 2-layer GCN is to balance simplicity and expressive power to model spatial information. The 2-layer GCN model with input node feature matrix V and adjacency matrix A can be expressed as:

$$f(V, A) = \text{ReLU}(\widetilde{A} \, \text{ReLU}(\widetilde{A}VW_0)W_1), \qquad (3)$$

where $\widetilde{A} = \hat{D}^{-\frac{1}{2}} \hat{A} \hat{D}^{-\frac{1}{2}}$ denotes the normalized adjacency matrix with $\hat{A} = A + I$ is a normalized adjacency matrix that adds self-loops to the original graph and $\hat{D}$ is the diagonal degree matrix of $\hat{A}$. $W_0 \in \mathbb{R}^{C \times H}$ denotes the weight matrix from input to the first hidden layer, $W_1 \in \mathbb{R}^{H \times F}$ represents the weight matrix from the hidden layer to the output, $f(V, A) \in \mathbb{R}^{N \times F}$ represents the output with sequence length F, and ReLU($\cdot$) is rectified linear unit, an activation function.

The two graphs are modelled parallelly: $f(V, A^{\text{filtered}})$ and $f(V, A^{\text{optimal}})$. Since the brain classification task is based on graph-level classification, we need to implement a *graph pooling* operator for both graph embeddings. The CONCAT pooling operator combines all node embeddings into a single vector to maintain overall information. Two vectors are generated from graph pooling implementation: $\hat{z}^{\text{filtered}} = \text{POOL}(f(V, A^{\text{filtered}}))$ and $\hat{z}^{\text{optimal}} = \text{POOL}(f(V, A^{\text{optimal}}))$.

3.3   Classifier

Once we get the graph representation $\hat{z}^{\text{filtered}}$ and $\hat{z}^{\text{optimal}}$, we perform concatenation to combine the information from both spatial information as follows: $(\hat{z}^{\text{filtered}} || \hat{z}^{\text{optimal}})$. Then we apply two fully connected layers to implement binary disease classification so that is: $y = \text{FC}(\text{FC}(\hat{z}^{\text{filtered}} || \hat{z}^{\text{optimal}}))$. The output y is mapped into 1, indicating a specific brain disease or 0 for a normal sample.

4   Experiment

In this experiment section, we aim to answer 3 research questions: **RQ1**: Does Bargrain outperform baseline methods in terms of accuracy for brain disease detection? **RQ2**: Do various components in Bargrain contribute to the overall model performance? **RQ3**: Are there underlying differences between the two kinds of graph structures employed in Bargrain model to use as complementary information?

4.1   Datasets

We conduct experiments with 3 open-source fMRI brain classification datasets: First, Cobre[2] records fMRI data from 72 patients with schizophrenia and 75 healthy controls. We preprocessed the Cobre dataset with 150 temporal signal steps and 96 ROI nodes. Second, ACPI[3] records fMRI data to classify 62 patients with marijuana consumption records and 64 with healthy controls. We preprocessed the ACPI dataset with 700 temporal signal steps and 200 ROI nodes. Third, ABIDE [4] records fMRI data from 402 patients with autism and 464 healthy controls. We preprocessed the ABIDE dataset with 192 temporal signal steps and 111 ROI nodes.

4.2   Baseline Approaches and Reproducibility

We compare the performance of our proposed method with the latest brain disease detection frameworks such as FBNetGNN [10], DGM [13], BrainNetCNN [12], BrainNETTF [11] and GDC-GCN [5]. We used their original code implementations to carry out the experiment.

4.3   Model Selection and Experiment Setup

We divide each data set into training sets (80%) and testing sets (20%). Furthermore, we again split the training sets into actual training sets (85%) and validation sets (15%) to help model selections.

We used AMD Rayzen 7 5800H @ 3.20 GHz with NVIDIA GeForce RTX 3050 Ti GPU to run the experiments. The model was trained by Adam optimizer with

---

[2] http://cobre.mrn.org/.
[3] http://fcon_1000.projects.nitrc.org/indi/ACPI/html/.

a learning rate 1×10^{-4}. In the first layer GCN, we used a 256 embedding size for Cobre and ACPI, and 64 for ABIDE. In the second layer GCN, we used 256 embedding sizes for Cobre and ACPI, and 512 for ABIDE. To ensure the sparsity of the filtered correlation matrix graph, we set 0.6 as a threshold c. Moreover, we configured $\tau = 1$ for the temperature in the Gumbel reparameterization trick.

4.4   RQ1. Performance Comparison

The brain disease classification results on three datasets are presented in table 1. Our model achieved the best with an average F1-score of 0.7329 across three datasets. By incorporating both actual domain knowledge and optimal structure graph information, Bargrain is able to enhance classification performance. Compared with the methods that solely rely on domain knowledge graphs, such as GDC-GCN, and the techniques that only use optimal graph structure, such as DGM, our approach outperforms them in classifying brain disease. However, it should be noted that our balanced structure graphs do not necessarily reduce the model complexity since we combine both types of information. Furthermore, There is potential for further research to explore optimizing the efficiency of models while maintaining a balance between those two graph structures and performing incremental learning when there is a concept drift in the current knowledge [7].

Table 1. The experiment results based on F1 score, sensitivity, specificity, and area under the receiver operating characteristic curve (ROC/AUC).

Methods	Cobre				ACPI				ABIDE				Average F1
	F1	Sens	Spec	AUC	F1	Sens	Spec	AUC	F1	Sens	Spec	AUC	
FBNetGNN	0.5600	0.5000	0.7333	0.6167	0.6000	0.7500	0.3077	0.5288	0.6486	0.6383	0.6173	0.6278	0.6029
DGM	0.6400	0.5714	0.8000	0.6857	0.7200	0.7500	**0.6923**	0.7212	0.5631	0.617	0.3333	0.4752	0.6410
BrainNetCNN	0.6923	0.6429	0.8000	0.7214	0.5833	0.5833	0.6154	0.5994	0.7158	0.7234	**0.6543**	**0.6889**	0.6638
BrainNETTF	0.5217	0.4286	0.8000	0.6143	0.6400	0.6667	0.6154	0.6410	0.6984	0.7021	0.6420	0.6721	0.6200
GDC-GCN	0.5185	0.5000	0.6000	0.5500	0.6250	0.8333	0.2308	0.5321	0.6377	0.7021	0.4198	0.5609	0.5937
Bargrain	**0.7407**	**0.7143**	0.8000	**0.7571**	**0.7407**	0.8333	0.6154	**0.7244**	0.7172	**0.7553**	0.5926	0.674	**0.7329**

4.5   RQ2. Ablation Studies

We evaluate the effectiveness of the components of our model. To do this, we perform ablation studies by excluding specific components of our model. There are three ablation settings. We exclude each graph structure and instead maintain only one graph structure. First, without the filtered correlation matrix graph (*-CorrGraph*) and second, without the optimal sampling graph (*-OptimGraph*). The last is without graph convolution (*-GConv*), which removes the graph embedding process.

The results of the ablation studies, presented in Table 2, demonstrate that the most effective components for improving brain disease detection performance within the Bargrain framework are the full framework components.

4.6   RQ.3 Brain's Graph Structure Interpretation

This section presents visualizations highlighting the characteristic differences between the two types of graph structures. In terms of their relationship characteristics (refer to Subsect. 3.2), the filtered correlation matrix exhibits an undirected structure, while the optimal sampling graph has a directed structure. Additionally, Fig. 2.a presents visualizations of two distinct brain graph structures from a single person in the Cobre dataset. For visualization purposes, we randomly selected the top 2% generated edges within each brain network type. A noticeable difference emerges: the optimal sampling graph tends to have a denser graph than the filtered correlation matrix, which brings another information perspective.

Table 2. Ablation Studies.

Methods	F1			Average F1
	Cobre	ACPI	ABIDE	
Bargrain	**0.7407**	**0.7407**	**0.7172**	**0.7329**
- *CorrGraph*	0.6923	0.6667	0.6845	0.6812
- *OptimGraph*	0.6923	0.6086	0.5028	0.6012
- *GConv*	0.6400	0.6086	0.6588	0.6358

Filtered Correlation Matrix Graph   Optimal Sampling Graph

(a) For visualization purposes, we randomly choose the top 2% of edges to display.

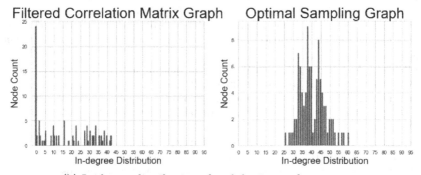

(b) In-degree distribution of each brain graph structure.

Fig. 2. Balanced graph structure interpretation for a person in the Cobre dataset.

Furthermore, as depicted in Fig. 2.b, these graphs exhibit distinct variations in their in-degree distributions, indicating the number of edges entering a specific node. The optimal sampling graph displays a bell-shaped distribution around the mid-range, with most nodes having in-degree edges ranging from 35 to 45. Notably, all nodes within the optimal sampling graph maintain connections with other nodes, unlike the filtered correlation matrix graph showing some nodes without connection.

Leveraging the diverse insights from both graphs is the primary goal of Bargrain. Thus, based on those interpretations, integrating those structures within the learning model becomes necessary to enhance prediction accuracy.

5   Conclusion

We proposed a brain disease detection method called **Bargrain** (balanced graph structure for brains). It employs two graph generation techniques: a filtered correlation matrix and an optimal sampling graph. Modeling those two graph representations balances the domain knowledge structure based on actual biological insight and the learnable optimal structure to prevent some noisy relations. Our method demonstrates a great performance compared to the state-of-the-art models, as shown in our extensive experiment. In our future works, we desire to implement a data-efficient approach to reduce the complexity of models for having dense relations based on high numbers of nodes in brain networks.

References

1. Chen, W., Wang, Y., Du, C., Jia, Z., Liu, F., Chen, R.: Balanced spatial-temporal graph structure learning for multivariate time series forecasting: a trade-off between efficiency and flexibility. In: ACML. PMLR (2023)
2. Cui, H., et al.: Braingb: a benchmark for brain network analysis with graph neural networks. IEEE Trans. Med. Imaging **42**(2), 493–506 (2022)
3. Dadi, K., et al.: Benchmarking functional connectome-based predictive models for resting-state FMRI. Neuroimage **192**, 115–134 (2019)
4. Di Martino, A., et al.: The autism brain imaging data exchange: towards a large-scale evaluation of the intrinsic brain architecture in autism. Mol. Psychiatry **19**(6), 659–667 (2014)
5. ElGazzar, A., Thomas, R., Van Wingen, G.: Benchmarking graph neural networks for FMRI analysis. arXiv preprint arXiv:2211.08927 (2022)
6. Febrinanto, F.G.: Efficient graph learning for anomaly detection systems. In: Proceedings of the Sixteenth ACM International Conference on Web Search and Data Mining, pp. 1222–1223 (2023)
7. Febrinanto, F.G., Xia, F., Moore, K., Thapa, C., Aggarwal, C.: Graph lifelong learning: a survey. IEEE Comput. Intell. Mag. **18**(1), 32–51 (2023)
8. Hutchison, R.M., et al.: Dynamic functional connectivity: promise, issues, and interpretations. Neuroimage **80**, 360–378 (2013)
9. Jang, E., Gu, S., Poole, B.: Categorical reparameterization with gumbel-softmax. In: International Conference on Learning Representations (ICLR) (2017)

10. Kan, X., Cui, H., Lukemire, J., Guo, Y., Yang, C.: FBNetGen: task-aware GNN-based FMRI analysis via functional brain network generation. In: MIDL. PMLR (2022)
11. Kan, X., Dai, W., Cui, H., Zhang, Z., Guo, Y., Yang, C.: Brain network transformer. In: Advances in Neural Information Processing Systems (NeurIPS) (2022)
12. Kawahara, J., et al.: BrainNetCNN: convolutional neural networks for brain networks; towards predicting neurodevelopment. Neuroimage **146**, 1038–1049 (2017)
13. Kazi, A., Cosmo, L., Ahmadi, S.A., Navab, N., Bronstein, M.M.: Differentiable graph module (DGM) for graph convolutional networks. IEEE Trans. Pattern Anal. Mach. Intell. **45**(2), 1606–1617 (2022)
14. Li, X., et al.: BrainGNN: interpretable brain graph neural network for FMRI analysis. Med. Image Anal. **74**, 102233 (2021)
15. Ren, J., Xia, F., Lee, I., Noori Hoshyar, A., Aggarwal, C.: Graph learning for anomaly analytics: algorithms, applications, and challenges. ACM Trans. Intell. Syst. Technol. **14**(2), 1–29 (2023)
16. Shang, C., Chen, J., Bi, J.: Discrete graph structure learning for forecasting multiple time series. In: International Conference on Learning Representations (ICLR) (2020)
17. Welling, M., Kipf, T.N.: Semi-supervised classification with graph convolutional networks. In: International Conference on Learning Representations (ICLR) (2017)
18. Xia, F., et al.: CenGCN: centralized convolutional networks with vertex imbalance for scale-free graphs. IEEE Trans. Knowl. Data Eng. **35**(5), 4555–4569 (2022)

Author Index

© The Editor(s) (if applicable) and The Author(s), under exclusive license
to Springer Nature Singapore Pte Ltd. 2023
S. Wu et al. (Eds.): PKAW 2023, LNAI 14317, pp. 145–146, 2023.
https://doi.org/10.1007/978-981-99-7855-7

Printed in the United States
by Baker & Taylor Publisher Services

Printed in the United States
by Baker & Taylor Publisher Services